# PEAKE
## IN
# CHINA

Dec 1949

# PEAKE IN CHINA

## Memoirs of Ernest Cromwell Peake

With an Introduction by Hilary Spurling

THE BRITISH LIBRARY

First published in 2014 by

The British Library
96 Euston Road
London NW1 2DB

*Memoirs of a Doctor in China* copyright ©
The Estate of Dr Ernest Cromwell Peake 2014

Introduction copyright © Hilary Spurling 2014

Illustrations copyright © The Estate of Dr Ernest Cromwell
Peake 2014, except for the following: p. 2 copyright
© The Estate of Mervyn Peake 2014; pp. 10, 12 (below),
21, 28 copyright © Mu Dehuah 2014

Half-title: the Peake family in China
Frontispiece: Ernest Cromwell Peake,
drawing by Mervyn Peake

British Library Cataloguing-in-Publication Data
A catalogue record for this book is available
from the British Library

ISBN 978 0 7123 5741 8

Designed and typeset by
Briony Hartley, Goldust Design

Printed in Malta by Gutenberg Press

# CONTENTS

*Mervyn Peake in China, c.1919*

# NOTE TO THE READER

This book presents, for the first time, the memoirs by Dr Ernest Peake (1874–1950), father of Mervyn Peake, relating to his years as a medical missionary in China at the turn of the twentieth century. The typescript of the memoirs is held in the British Library (Add MS 88931/6/2) as part of the Mervyn Peake Archive.

## CHINESE POLITICS AT THE TURN OF THE TWENTIETH CENTURY

Dr Peake's account of his time in China spans a period of acute turmoil and change. 1899 was not an auspicious time to arrive and it was perhaps not an entirely responsible decision on the part of the London Missionary Society to send him just then. Though the danger from the rapidly growing Boxer movement was far more serious than anything seen before, it may have been viewed as just part of the apparently unending series of attacks to be borne by Christians. From the 1860s, every year there were attacks on missionaries and Chinese converts, sometimes individual attacks, sometimes wholesale burnings and killings. In 1860 Catholic churches, orphanages and converts' houses were attacked in Nanchang; in 1863, the Catholic cathedral in Chongqing was destroyed; in 1868, 10,000 people attacked the Protestant China Inland Mission houses in Yangzhou and a hundred Chinese Christians were murdered in Sichuan, and there were further attacks in Guizhou that year. In 1870, the French consulate, church and hospital in Tianjin were burnt, together with 100 orphans and nuns. In 1873 an American church was attacked in Ruichang and Catholic missionaries and converts died in Qianjing. There were attacks on both Protestants and Catholics in Wuhu and Ichang on the Yangtze in 1891 and a massacre of Christians in Gucheng in 1895, as well as attacks in Sichuan and Fujian. As well as further attacks in Sichuan and Yunnan in 1899, that year saw a massive increase of violence in Shandong [Shantung] province as the Boxer revolt grew in strength. Dr Peake felt hostility in Heng-chow [Hengyang] but made no mention of the Boxer threat from his position 'away in distant Hunan' until the local magistrate, responsible for his safety, took precautions.

The difference between Hengyang in 1898 and Tianjin after 1912 is dramatic. It was not just that Tianjin was a cosmopolitan city with a well-equipped hospital but also that life for foreigners in China had changed. The Republic of China was outward-looking, keen to modernise and to adopt Western ways, and the annual series of attacks on isolated foreign missionaries was a thing of the past.

## NAMES AND SPELLING

Dr Peake's memoir uses the old Wade-Giles system of romanising Chinese names and terms. Modern readers are likely to be more familiar with the pinyin system, and pinyin versions of Chinese words have therefore been inserted into the memoir in square brackets where they may help to clarify Dr Peake's references.

## FOOTNOTES

Notes in the memoir come from two sources:
[ECP] indicates a note in the original typescript by Ernest Peake.
[FW] indicates a note by Dr Frances Wood, formerly Curator of Chinese Collections at the British Library, to clarify political and social contexts that may be unfamiliar to readers without a specialist interest in Chinese history.

## ILLUSTRATIONS

Dr Peake's original typescript was illustrated by his son Mervyn, whose help he acknowledged thus: 'I am indebted to my younger son Mervyn for the illustrations, which have caught so faithfully the atmosphere of by-gone days in a fascinating country'. The illustrations in this edition are principally Dr Peake's own photographs and postcards from his collection.

# INTRODUCTION
## Hilary Spurling

### FATHER AND SON

The careers of both Ernest Peake and his son, the writer and artist Mervyn Peake, were fired and shaped by China. Shipped out as a newly qualified young doctor by the London Missionary Society in 1899, Dr Peake set up a medical practice serving an area roughly the size of England in southern Hunan, where Western medicine was still unknown. After a decade of successful expansion, he left to run the only hospital for Chinese people in the northern city of Tientsin [Tianjin]. Mervyn spent his first eleven years in Tientsin, sailing for the UK at the end of 1922 with a store of images that would exert a powerful pull ever after on one of the strongest and strangest imaginations of his English generation.

A key resource for father and son was the mountain refuge called Kuling [Guling] on Lushan in Chiang-hsi [Jiangxi]. One of China's most venerable ancient mountains, a hump-backed, sheer-sided range rising nearly five thousand feet above sea level from the sweltering plains of the Yang-tse [Yangtze] valley, Lushan had been a beauty spot visited by writers, painters, scholars, monks and emperors for more than two thousand years before it was annexed at the end of the nineteenth century by Western missionaries. Their settlement was part sanctuary, part sanatorium, laid out like an English garden suburb on gently sloping woodland between three wooded pinnacles in 1896.[1] To Dr Peake, arriving three years later as part of the first wave of British visitors, Kuling seemed a 'wise and humane institution'.[2]

9

*Lushan in Chiang-hsi (Jiangxi), the mountain where Dr Peake first met his wife, and where their son Mervyn was born.*

He was twenty-three years old, disorientated and already suffering from the kind of tensions that would by his own account[3] grow worse as he moved further into regions that remained for Europeans uncharted territory. Most missionaries initially experienced something similar, recoiling like Peake with incredulity bordering on panic from the ferocious energy that made street life in Chinese cities look and sound more like a riot. Westerners found it impossible to escape the inquisitive derision of bystanders fingering their clothes, testing out their skin pigment, keeping up a running commentary on their strangely coloured eyes and hair. Active hostility was never far below the surface. Missionaries got used to being greeted with sticks, stones and feral dogs. Peake was not the first to spend months holed up indoors in an inland town, unable to explore the streets except in a dark, stuffy, tightly closed sedan chair. Extreme humidity in the south coupled with summer temperatures in the mid-thirties by day and night made work difficult, and sleep next to impossible. Cholera and malaria raged up and down the Yang-tse valley. Political disturbance was endemic. Attempts at Western-style modernisation had been suspended, shortly before Peake's arrival, after a violent crisis that was still working itself out in a highly volatile atmosphere of rumour and reprisal with the severed heads of reformers prominently on display ('I myself, in Hunan, saw one hoisted on the top of a pole'). Xenophobia erupted nationwide the year after, raising vengeful mobs even in Hunan, causing much of the mission community to retreat downriver to the coast, and provoking swift retaliation in the form of Allied military intervention, and Chinese defeat reinforced by a punitive and humiliating peace treaty.

Kuling offered refuge from danger, pollution and contagion as well as from the sheer press and ceaseless din of people shouting, quarrelling, cursing or simply advertising goods for sale by day, and beating gongs or exploding fire crackers at night to scare off marauding spirits. Lushan's clear streams and clean fresh air signalled a drop of ten degrees after the steamy heat of the rice-fields on the plain below. Many young missionaries met future partners there as Peake did in 1903. After a year in China, Elizabeth Powell had developed lung problems so severe that she was under doctor's orders to leave for a more temperate climate in

*Top: Kuling, Mervyn's birthplace, laid out by missionaries in the 1890s to resemble an English garden suburb on top of Lushan.*

*Bottom: South-east face of Lushan rising like a fortress from the flatlands below.*

South Africa[4] when she retreated to convalesce in Kuling, and married Ernest Peake instead. Her health remained precarious, not helped by a job as matron in her husband's hospital, but kept more or less stable by summers on the mountain virtually every year until the family left Hunan. Kuling was 'a life-saving station', according to a fellow missionary.[5] 'One cannot help feeling well there,' said Bessie Peake.[6]

Sporadic outbreaks of unrest increased after the Dowager-Empress died in 1908, leaving a two-year-old boy installed on the imperial throne of the Manchus. The Peakes' elder son, Leslie, was put into a Kuling school as a boarder aged six in 1911 for safety's sake. Their second son, Mervyn, was born on the mountain that July. The family was still there in October when serious protest in Wuchang, followed by fierce fighting at Hankow (Dr Peake joined the Red Cross on the front line), precipitated a tide of insurrection throughout China that ended only with the abdication of the Manchu emperor, and the inauguration of the first Chinese Republic. Mervyn was carried down the mountain aged five months that winter. The Peakes spent the following summer in Kuling before moving reluctantly to the distant north, 'a dry and weary land', where Mervyn grew up hearing stories of Lushan's cool grottoes, deep pools and shady trees. He revisited the mountain once more aged eight and was enchanted by it, swimming, picnicking and exploring its stony heights on a family holiday in the summer of 1919.[7] A quarter of a century later in the first two books of an extraordinary trilogy – *Titus Groan*, *Gormenghast* and *Titus Alone* – he would recreate Mount Lu, or what he called its imaginative residue,[8] as the towering cone of Gormenghast Mountain with its crags and gorges, its mist-covered flanks, its caves, lakes, woods, and its precipitous peaks.

## ERNEST CROMWELL PEAKE

When Dr Peake landed in Shanghai in February, 1899, the first thing he noted was the bright colours – glazed roof-tiles glinting in the sunshine and small boys on the ramparts, 'very quaint in their loose garments and little pigtails', flying painted paper kites shaped like dragons, fish and crocodiles. It was a startling sight (contemporary Western children wore white – the colour of mourning in China – until they were old enough at four or five to put on the dark, tight-fitting clothes that encased them neck to toe from then on). In Peake's recollections written nearly half a century later, the jostling crush on the streets and the unfriendliness of the citizens were relegated to second place by the bold little boys flying their gaudy and inventive kites from the top of the city wall.

Peake and his future wife belonged to a generation of enterprising, ambitious, idealistic young people for whom China represented unlimited opportunity. It was not simply that the more adventurous missionaries explored regions few other Westerners had ever penetrated. They could expect an extraordinary degree of autonomy, independence and responsibility as they set out to establish distant bases, travelling frequently alone or with a single companion, equipped after basic local training with rudimentary knowledge of the language but little or no concept of the cultural, political and social norms, let alone the religious traditions of the people they planned to save. In theory these young missionaries were closely monitored, but in practice supervision was exercised by district committees based often hundreds of miles away whose advice and instructions sometimes took weeks to arrive by slow and complicated canal and river transport.

Peake's memoirs skip his own three-year preparatory period, presumably because he thought of himself as marking time while he studied theology, learned Chinese and worked under other doctors in mission centres already established on the Yang-tse river in Hankow [Hankou] and Yochow [Yueyang].[9] In fact it was not until the spring of 1902 that he finally got his posting to Hengchow [Hengyang], over a thousand miles by water from Shanghai, reached by a slow house boat propelled by river boatmen four hundred miles up one of the Yang-tse's tributaries to the junction where it met all the southern rivers of Hunan. It was 'the great centre for the trade of the south', according to Peake,[10] who had already earmarked Hengchow as the headquarters of a future Hunan mission. For the moment he found himself one of three protestant missionaries in a city of roughly a quarter of a million people, who received him without enthusiasm 'in silence and stupefaction'.

Himself the child of missionary parents in Madagascar, Peake had been educated as a boarder at an English mission college before enrolling at medical school in Edinburgh.[11] His background made him more realistic, perhaps more aware, certainly far more experienced than contemporaries with no first-hand knowledge of the mission field. The imperatives that drove other missionaries – apt to be overwhelmed by the unimaginable numbers of damned souls due for salvation – oppressed Peake far less than the need for practical solutions. Outsize goitres, malignant tumours, swollen bladders and distended bellies, smallpox, beri-beri and elephantiasis bore down unchecked on the population. Grotesquely heavy weights were routinely shifted by men rather than by carts or wagons, working singly or in human transport convoys, doubled over under loads that twisted spines, wore out joints at shoulder, hip and knee, and made tendons stand out like corded ropes of wire.

When Peake opened the first hospital in Hengchow, in practice a makeshift clinic with dispensary attached, just over thirty patients turned up each day for treatment.[12] He was still met with scowls and death threats on the street, but patient numbers rose little by little year by year. He planned a new hospital, and sent off repeated, unanswered pleas for a trained nurse. Resources were strictly limited, and the local helpers he trained himself could not be relied on for much more than routine jobs. The total lack of sanitation in a town with open sewers and lepers on the streets dismayed him. It was 'slow, discouraging, uphill work', he wrote in his annual report for 1903. Most potential patients still preferred to entrust their healing to the local gods, who could be propitiated with sacrifices, or abused and put out to blister in the sun if things went wrong. Deformed, sick or broken bodies had to be beaten to drive out the evil spirits who had done the damage in the first place. Devils in possession of dysfunctional body parts were skewered with dirty needles ('Countless eyes have been ruined by needle puncture'[13]). The surgeon's knife inspired such terror that for years the six beds in Peake's surgical ward stood empty.

The turning point was a cataract operation performed on a prominent citizen who had gone blind in his seventies. Peake knew well enough that his future, and perhaps his safety, depended on the outcome.

The successful result had a magical aftermath that became a Peake family legend. Shortly after his first attempt at surgery, the doctor and his Chinese assistant were surprised to see a procession in the street outside, 'a long single file of bedraggled and apparently dejected men ... with heads bowed and shoulders bent.... each man had hold of the pigtail of the one immediately in front of him'.[14] The local blind men were heading for the hospital, led by the doctor's newly sighted patient whose gratitude took the form of a spectacularly successful PR stunt. The new hospital Peake opened in 1905 had an annual intake of six or seven thousand within five years.

In the decade he spent in Hunan, Peake developed administrative, fund-raising and training skills as well as a natural talent for man management. He had no proselytising instinct, and none of the self-righteous religiosity that makes so many mission memoirs hard to take today. He rarely used the patronising clichés of his age ('such was the thick darkness in which the people groped'[15]), and even then only in the context of the superstitions that made his work much harder. After a tricky start, he clearly liked and got on well with the Chinese, whom he himself came in some ways to resemble. He shared their earthy sense of humour as well as their innate courtesy and patience. He was kind, gentle, slow-spoken, and known universally, even to his family, as Doc. His wife, a small, dark, lively Welsh girl who sang and played the piano, proved an indefatigable assistant. It is not hard to see why his mission superiors insisted on transferring him, in spite of strenuous pleas and arguments, to revitalise a failing hospital in the north in 1912.[16]

Founded by General Gordon as a flagship for the Western medical community in 1861, Tientsin's Mackenzie Memorial Hospital was now in need of radical overhaul. On a preliminary visit of inspection, Peake found the premises inadequate, most of the staff in need of replacement, funds as usual scarce and patient numbers low. 'It is a pretty hopeless and thankless task you have set me', he wrote angrily that autumn to a committee that remained adamant.[17] Grumbling that his allowance for expenses would not even cover the cost of furs for the whole family in the sub-zero temperatures of a Tientsin winter, Peake set out in December with his wife, six-year-old Leslie and the infant Mervyn on a journey of a thousand miles that took four weeks. The two boys would grow up in Tientsin while their father reorganised medical and surgical facilities for the city's Chinese population. In the ten years of his tenure, the hospital's annual turnover rose to nearly forty thousand out-patients with well over a thousand major operations performed each year by Peake and his Chinese deputy, Dr Lei. Ambitious plans for a new hospital had to be set aside when Mrs Peake developed ominous signs of heart trouble in 1922, necessitating urgent return and eventual settlement in England for the whole family. By the time Peake's spacious modern buildings were finally erected in Tientsin, he had left to spend the rest of his working life as a country doctor at Wallington in Surrey.

China meanwhile relapsed further into a chaotic anarchy that would only partially abate with the establishment of a Nationalist government in 1927. Peake's first direct experience of serious disorder had been the revolt of 1900 (generally known as the Boxer uprising), when he tended sick and sometimes grossly injured refugees in a climate of such risk and tension that he had to employ thirty men to guard his house that winter,[18] long after hostilities had been forcibly suppressed. 'Peace covered China like a sheet of thin ice beneath which a river boiled,' as an older missionary said.[19] When the empire fell apart almost of its own volition eleven years later, Peake left his two little sons with their mother in Kuling to join the small band of Red Cross mission doctors who witnessed at first hand the last defiant spasm of the dying Manchu Dynasty as its army routed resistance fighters at Hankow. He dressed their horrific wounds, and recorded what was happening in images − dead bodies littering the battlefield beside the river, a looter's head slung up as a warning on the street − that vividly convey the squalor and pathos of the fighting. He photographed belching black smoke over Hankow as the city burned, the destruction of the viceroy's palace at Wuchang, and the steam-boat he and his colleagues commandeered to rescue the dead and dying from their blood-soaked sampans after imperial shellfire raked civilians attempting to flee. It was the climactic episode of a career that saw China forever on the brink of political implosion and economic collapse, powerless to prevent its own military disintegration or resist the European powers that took the opportunity to carve up its territory.

Written more than twenty years after his return to England, Peake's recollections touch only briefly on this turbulent background, and remain studiously reticent about himself and his family. His brief survey of political and historical events in chapters 10–12 reflects the standard assumptions of his time, heavily skewed in both China and the West by misinformation and hostile contemporary propaganda. Peake's approval of the young emperor, and highly critical view of the Empress-Dowager as malevolent, backward-looking and implacably opposed to reform – views shared in his day by most other people, including the British Foreign Office – have had to be more or less reversed a century later in the light of previously inaccessible documentation, much of it emanating from Chinese imperial archives only in the last two or three decades.[20]

The historical interest of these memoirs lies in Peake's first-hand experience through work. He confronted on a daily basis the effects of superstition, ignorance, dirt, malnutrition, pollution and infection. In the rapidly expanding and modernising city of Tientsin, he encountered macabre injuries inflicted on people unused to motorised and rail traffic, or to the industrial machinery that gouged and mangled flesh, crushed bones, ripped off limbs, once even scalped a careless operator. The galvanic changes sweeping China are reflected in his text in a medical microcosm, not through their broad external consequences, but in their immediate and intimate impact on the long-suffering human body. Peake constructs his narrative with the clarity and precision of early scientific training. Its testimony is authentic, its detail incisive and surprising, its tone practical, engaging and humane, like the man himself.

## MERVYN PEAKE

'To north, south, east or west, turning at will, it was not long before his landmarks fled him.'[21] *Titus Alone,* the last volume of Mervyn Peake's *Gormenghast* trilogy, starts with the young Titus Groan abandoning the mountain that was the only world he had ever known. The disorientation of the novel's opening sentence looks back to Peake's eleven-year-old self at the end of 1922 when he, too, lost the only world he knew on leaving China to settle with his family in England. The book ends with the adult Titus realising on the last page that, no matter what he did or where he went, '*he carried his Gormenghast within him*'.

Memories of China haunt all three of Peake's novels. 'The pictures in my mind seem not to be a part of me, but are like the glimpses of some half-forgotten story in a book,' he wrote in the notebook where he jotted down recollections of his early years.[22] It was from these pictures, still pristine in their freshness and intensity, retrieved intact from a past in which he said he only half believed, that Peake began constructing in 1940 an alternative imaginative reality, where even the weather invokes the climate of his childhood. No English writer has more brilliantly conveyed the different properties of moonlight, sunlight, starlight, dusk and dawn, the brutal winter cold and torpid heat Mervyn had known as a boy in Tientsin, where temperatures could drop far below freezing and rise again a few months later to forty degrees. 'The sun ... was never more than a rayless disc this summer – in the thick hot air – a sick circle, unrefreshing and aloof', he wrote, describing a Gormenghast immobilised by 'this slow pulp of summer, this drag of heat, with the incurious yellow eye within it, floating monotonously, day after day', relieved only by subtropical rain, 'falling from the sky in long, upright and seemingly motionless lines of rosy silver that stand rigidly upon the ground ...'[23] The dense white mists covering Lushan for two thirds of the year swathe Gormenghast as well. The great flood that devastated northern China in 1917, reducing the city of Tientsin to an urban promontory rising from a vast inland sea, reappears in the final chapters of *Gormenghast* when floodwaters almost submerge the mountain:

on the rocky slopes, not more than three hundred feet from the claw-like summit ... the castle could be seen heaving across the skyline like the sheer sea-wall of a continent; a seaboard nibbled with countless coves and bitten deep with shadowy embayments. A continent, off whose shores the crowding islands lay; islands of every shape that towers can be; and archipelagos; and isthmuses and bluffs; and stark peninsulas of wandering stone – an inexhaustible panorama whose every detail was mirrored in the breathless flood below.[24]

The Peakes lived inside the London Missionary Society's walled compound in Tientsin's French concession in one of six identical Victorian mission houses that 'had no business to be in China. They might well have been flown over, all in a row, from Croydon'.[25] Intended as a haven for people struggling to retain their identity in an alien context, the compound seemed to Mervyn in retrospect drab and ugly, almost a parody of suburban conformity and security. He felt the same about Tientsin grammar school, designed expressly to replicate the customs, mentality and myths of the British education system. But he rode to school on his donkey every day past 'huts outside the compound, where the poorest lived, and the stray dogs, scrawny with hunger, sniffed and dug and scratched...'[26] The foreign community in their adjacent concessions had electricity and running water in spacious buildings with deep shady verandahs laid out along tree-lined avenues. A million people crammed into the cramped narrow overhanging and insanitary streets of the Chinese city. Like most mission children, Mervyn learned Mandarin from his Chinese amah at the same time as he started speaking English with his parents.[27] Unlike them, he knew from the inside the world of amahs, houseboys, cooks and cleaners, market stall-holders and bearers, people 'bitter with poverty and prone to those diseases that thrive on squalor', who lived on the far side of high walls put up to protect the privileged inmates from contact with people outside, 'as though to keep out a plague'.[28] Scant diet and hard labour meant that these people grew old prematurely. 'No one looked middle-aged. The mothers were ... as ancient in appearance as their own parents ... Only their children had radiance, their eyes, the sheen on their hair ... their movements and their voices ...'[29]

All these descriptions come from Peake's account of the Outer Dwellers living with their scavenging feral dogs in mud huts clamped to the stones of Gormenghast, overlapping one another and breasting up against the castle's massive outer walls just as the shelters made by

20

*Lushan's famous 'sea of clouds', never forgotten by Mervyn Peake; 'slow lack-lustre veils descend over Gormenghast. The mountain appeared and disappeared a score of times during the morning as the drifts obscured it or lifted from its sides ...'*

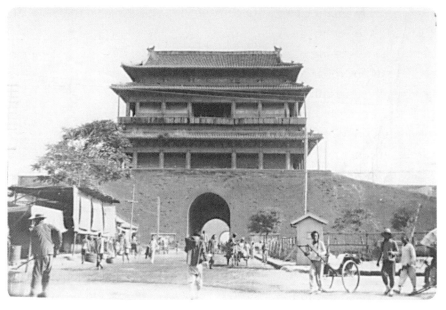

Outer and inner gates in Peking's city wall.

the poor from earth or straw clung to the ramparts of Chinese cities. The most monolithic of these walls surrounded the imperial city of Peking [Beijing], which was in fact three concentric walled cities, one inside the other. Tientsin was Peking's port, seventy miles downriver, and Mervyn shared his father's fascination with the ancient capital, and with the most secret of its inner enclaves, the Forbidden City, known to the Chinese as the 'Great Within', seat of a government as mysterious to its own people as to foreigners like Peake: 'The "Great Within" represented the absolute authority and sovereignty of the state, the nerve-centre of autocratic government ... it also featured a depraved medieval court, functioning exactly as it had done for many centuries.'[30] It remained a closely guarded sanctum even after its power had passed to a Republican government. Mervyn was a small child when his father obtained a special permit to visit with a group of other doctors, bringing home pictures of imperial palaces, temples and lotus lakes. The Forbidden City still housed the deposed emperor, a helpless hostage from infancy to the tyranny of ritual, and just five years older than Mervyn, who grew up poring over the photos in his father's album, and listening to his father's tales of 'the young Emperor, a very intelligent boy, longing to be outside and to see something of the world ... virtually a prisoner within the walls of the "Great Within"'.

These stories fed long afterwards into the arcane ancestral rites and ceremonies of Gormenghast, performed under protest by the heir, Titus Groan, another rebellious lonely boy desperate to escape the grip of an ineluctable and oppressive past. The castle built high on Gormenghast mountain − a castle that seems with its 'long notched outline',[31] its spiky pinnacles and stony sides to be at times almost indistinguishable from the mountain itself − has Chinese as well as gothic roots. Its most obvious source was probably the great moated medieval grange of Arundel Castle in Sussex, looming across the river above the village of Lower Warningcamp, where the Peakes were living in 1940 when the first of the three novels took shape. But the Chinese strongholds Mervyn had known as a child also had their moats and mighty walls, their battlements, watch-towers, gate-houses, courtyards and fantastic roofscapes. He equipped Gormenghast with crumbling state rooms

Carved stone figures guarding the approach
to the Ming imperial tombs outside Peking.

very like the high-ceilinged, coloured and colonnaded halls of Chinese imperial power houses. The sculptures in its Hall of Bright Carvings recall the sharply observed and richly inventive stone animals that line the road to the imperial tombs outside Peking, or the ancient highway to Canton [Guangzhou] photographed by Dr Peake in 1903: 'grotesque figures reared their heads above the ground to stare at the foreign devil who had dared to intrude on their age-long solitude .... rampant lions, elephants, wild boars ... executed with great spirit. Many were weather-worn, tilted over at odd angles, and half buried in the ground...'

The father's memoirs are full of themes and figures that find a more substantial imaginative reality in the son's novels. In 1946, a few months after the end of China's brutal and protracted war with Japan, Dr Peake went back alone aged seventy-one to take charge of the only public hospital that had survived the occupation of Hong Kong. He had already started writing his memoirs, and he completed them after his return fourteen months later to an England itself still emerging battered and depleted from the second world war. Cut off from the West soon after the Communists came to power in 1949, China remained closed for the rest of Dr Peake's lifetime, and his son's.

He had brought back from Hong Kong a brush and ink-stone for Mervyn, who was already drawing in words with calligraphic delicacy and analytical precision in *Titus Groan*. Strangely enough, although his actual drawings belong to a classic English tradition with no discernible trace of oriental influence, the Gormenghast landscapes in his novels suggest that he had paid close attention to Chinese graphic art: 'the cedars, like great charcoal drawings, suddenly began to expose their structure, the layers of flat foliage rising tier above tier, their edges ribbed with sunrise', he wrote near the beginning of volume one, and, of a patch of moonlit scrub towards the end: 'Every blade of the grass was of consequence, and the few scattered stones held an authority that made their solid, separate marks upon the brain – each one with its own undu-plicated shape: each rising brightly from the ink of its own spilling.'[32]

After the family exodus in 1922, Mervyn himself never saw China again until he opened a cache of stored images in his mind and began the first draft of *Titus Groan*, soon after he had been called up in 1940 for basic army training as a gunner. He finished the book almost two years later during treatment in a military hospital for some kind of nervous collapse. Its spectacular set pieces – Swelter's invisible silent midnight pursuit of Flay, or the two breathtaking duels by moonlight – owe much to Chinese popular theatre. The physical extravagance of Peake's characters – Flay's slithering stride and cracking knees, the red-and-white scar tissue marbling Steerpike's burned face, Swelter's extreme nippiness on flat feet that suck at the stone floor like porridge – goes back to the malformed and misshapen bodies that had fascinated the young Mervyn in the operating theatre in Tientsin. He had acquired something of his father's scientific detachment and exactitude, heightened by a particular relish of his own in childhood when he watched at least one amputation and a dramatic tracheotomy.[33] He was a knowledgable and appreciative collector of operations performed by Dr Peake, who saved up his trickiest cases to pass on to Mervyn as well as documenting them in photo albums.[34]

Peake's Chinese years left their imprint on his imagination at every level. He made Titus's sister Fuchsia a connoisseur of the kind of weirdly convoluted tree roots, flints and fungi highly prized by Chinese collectors. He put the caged cormorants trained to fish in Chinese rivers into *Titus Alone*, just as he endowed Gormenghast with 'the high and jagged cone' of Lushan's summit, its woods of fir, chestnut and acacia, its twisted thorns and pine trees 'that leaned out fantastically into space',[35] its gorges falling sheer to the plain four thousand feet below. The marshlands at the foot of the mountain to the south have long since been drained, but seventy-five inches of rain still fall annually on Lushan, feeding the famous 'sea of clouds' considered by the Chinese one of its most memorable and mysterious assets. Peake returns again and again to the mists dropping from the sky or rising from the ground: 'slow, lack-lustre veils descended ... over Gormenghast.... The mountain appeared and disappeared a score of times during the morning as the drifts obscured it or lifted from its sides'.... 'From horizon to horizon it spread, this mist, supporting the massives of the mountain upon its foaming back, like a floating load of ugly crags and shale. It laid its fumes along the flanks of the mountain ...'[36]

26

Lushan's Cave of the Immortals, disputed for centuries between Buddhists and Daoists, opens out into a high, domed, circular space with projecting stone sills and ledges, overhung with ferns, and reached through a deep cleft in a hillside rising in tiers of shelving rock, like Flay's secret hideout in *Gormenghast*.[37] Many of the mountain's peaks are wooded, including Dahanyang, the highest of them all at 4,835 feet. Others take the form of rocky spines and escarpments, look-outs that command panoramic views of the surrounding plain. Lushan's inaccessibility, its sheer sides and cavernous recesses, make it a natural fortification that has sheltered many armies. Chiang Kai-shek, beset by challenges to his power, both internal and external, made it the Nationalists' summer capital in the 1930s and 40s. It was a prime target for the Japanese, whose army dislodged Kuomintang forces and occupied the mountain only after scouring out resistance by bombing from the air. In the 1950s Chairman Mao emphasised his presence with a monumental People's Hall, where the presidium met to witness famously sinister developments in 1959 and 1970.

It was Mao who built the fine road that now spirals up the mountain. Before that, summer residents had to be carried in flimsy rattan chairs slung on long bamboo poles by mountain bearers up an uneven stone staircase, and along narrow paths above ravines and chasms where the human cargo swung out into space. These were the Thousand Steps, 'the myriad steps like pavements' that Peake included on a list of key childhood images.[38] Many more thousands of these steps, carved into the rock, led to major sites like the Five Old Man Peak, five sandstone spires constructed from massive blocks of masonry sliced by geological shears and cleavers: 'Stone after grey stone', as Peake wrote of his castle, 'and a sense of the heaving skyward of great blocks, one upon another, in a climbing weight, ponderous and yet alive ...'[39] They form buttresses and towers, their sides pocked by openings and corbels, linked by winding passageways, and joined at one point between the third and fifth peaks by a mighty curving crenellated curtain wall of rock. Images lodged deep in Peake's imagination as a boy re-emerged twenty years later in the fictional stronghold of the Groans:

Top: Summit of Lushan where the whole vast range reaches its highest point, Dahanyang (far left).

Bottom: Five Old Man Peak on Lushan: 'a sense of heaving skyward of green blocks, one upon another in a climbing weight, ponderous and yet alive …'

The crumbling castle, looming among the mists, exhaled the season, and every cold stone breathed it out. The tortured trees by the dark lake burned and dripped, and their leaves snatched by the wind were whirled in wild circles through the towers. The clouds mouldered as they lay coiled, or shifted themselves uneasily upon the stone skyfield, sending up wreaths that drifted through the turrets and swarmed up the hidden walls.[40]

Of the nine hundred or more inscriptions carved into Lushan's rock walls by visitors, from the great third-century poet Tao Yuan-Ming to the first Ming Emperor and Chairman Mao in 1959, the lines most often quoted in China were written in the tenth century by Su Shi, in a poem about the way the mountain changes shape beneath its shifting veils of cloud: 'The true face of Lushan / I cannot see because I am in its midst.' It was a phenomenon that fascinated Peake who, like his father, both took from and gave back much to China. One of the more unexpected mission legacies is surely the addition of Mervyn Peake to the long line of visitors who have immortalised the changing faces of Lushan.

## NOTES

1 It was designed by a British missionary, Edward Selby Little, whose acquisition of the site, long held to be a triumph over heroic odds, looks by today's standards more like duplicity and graft (information from Susan Jakes, editor of ChinaFile, in an essay kindly supplied by Steve Harnsberger).

2 E. C. Peake's first annual report to the London Missionary Society, Jan/Feb 1900, LMS archive, School of Oriental and African Studies, London. ECP's letters, reports and related papers in this archive contain supplementary material missing from the memoir he wrote long afterwards; I am grateful to the editor of *Peake Studies*, Peter Winnington, for a detailed summary, cited hereafter as LMS.

3 23.6 and 5.9.1903, LMS.

4 Medical report, 19.3.1903, LMS.

5 Pearl Buck, see Hilary Spurling, *Burying the Bones: Pearl Buck in China*, 2010, pp. 27, 287.

6 Letter from E. Powell, 10.9.1903, LMS.

7 See John Watney, *Mervyn Peake*, 1976, p. 31, and *Peake's Progress*, ed. Maeve Gilmore, 1978, pp. 477, 480.

8  *Peake's Progress*, p. 47.

9  For these three years – March 1899 to April 1902 – see LMS.

10  Report, 27.11.1901, LMS; for the following quote, see below, p.57.

11  For the most reliable account of ECP's background, see Peter Winnington, *Mervyn Peake's Vast Alchemies: The Illustrated Biography*, 2009, p.25.

12  Annual report, 1901, LMS

13  See below, p.77.

14  See below, p.146.

15  See below, p.95.

16  The Hunan HQ was closed down, and the hospital sold to the American Presbyterian Mission: report of negotiations, May 1912, LMS.

17  22.9.1912, LMS.

18  Annual report 1900, LMS.

19  Pearl Buck, *My Several Worlds*, 1956, p. 64.

20  For a sympathetic and persuasive survey of current thinking, see Jung Chang, *Empress Dowager Cixi: The Concubine Who Launched Modern China*, 2013.

21  *Titus Alone*, 1968 [1950], p. 9.

22  *Peake's Progress*, p. 472.

23  *Titus Groan*, 1968 [1946], pp. 412 and 379.

24  *Gormenghast*, 1968 [1950], pp. 503–4.

25  *Peake's Progress*, p. 471.

26  Maeve Gilmore, *A World Away: A Memoir of Mervyn Peake*, 1970, p. 23.

27  Gordon Smith, *Mervyn Peake: A Personal Memoir*, 1984, p. 24.

28  *Gormenghast*, p. 278, and *Titus Groan*, p. 96.

29  *Titus Groan*, p. 92.

30  See below, p.100.

31  *Titus Groan*, p. 273.

32  *Titus Groan*, pp. 99, 281.

33  See Gordon Smith, *Mervyn Peake*, p. 22; *Peake's Progress*, p. 486

34  MP's early interest in surgical cases is documented in letters to him from ECP, 25.3. and 30.9.46, kindly shown me by Fabian Peake.

35  *Gormenghast*, pp. 503, 412; and see p. 131.

36  *Titus Groan*, p. 293; *Gormenghast*, p. 101.

37  *Gormenghast*, pp. 139–40, 412.

38  *Peake's Progress*, p. 477.

39  *Titus Groan*, p. 497.

40  *Titus Groan*, p. 196.

# MEMOIRS OF A DOCTOR IN CHINA

## Ernest Cromwell Peake

To the memory of my dear wife, and to my two sons,
both of whom were born in China, these memoirs
are affectionately dedicated.

# PREFACE

Fifty years ago, in 1898 the London Missionary Society was looking for a man to open up medical work in the closed province of Hunan in Central China.

I had recently graduated at Edinburgh University. I was free, and the prospect of undertaking a pioneering venture of this kind attracted me. I offered my services and was appointed for this particular enterprise.

Much water has flowed down the Yang-tse-Kiang [Yangtze river] following those far-off days; and it is now many years since I bade farewell to the Celestial Empire. During these later years great changes have been taking place. After untold ages dominated by immemorial usage and tradition, China is fast becoming 'modernised'. That is not *my* China. In these pages I write of the country and the people as I found them at the beginning of the present century.

At that time the Manchu Dynasty had held sway for close on 300 years, and the Empress-Dowager, seated on the Dragon Throne, ruled with the autocratic despotism of an Eastern potentate. In her ultra conservatism she was bitterly opposed to any suggestion of change. This, indeed was the attitude of the whole country. In her proud isolation China adopted a very superior pose, entertaining the utmost contempt for all foreign countries, and for all foreigners within her borders.

And yet, during the last two decades, China has been undergoing an astonishing metamorphosis. In the course of this short period she has, in some respects, leapt from Confucian times into the twentieth century.

Here in England one reads of railway development, aeroplane services, motor roads and 'bus routes'; and though one acknowledges the great benefits to be derived from petrol, electricity, and steam, it would not be the same China to me. I would miss the slow-moving house-boat, the sampan, the sedan-chair, the open palanquin, and even the squeaking wheel-barrow. I would probably be horrified by incompatible mixtures of East and West. Manners, I fear, would have lost much of their past-time courtesy, and the former charm would be gone.

It is in the desire to preserve something of my experiences in the old romantic China, and amidst a most interesting people, that these memories are recorded.

E.C.P.

# Chapter I

# ARRIVAL

It had always been my ambition to travel. I think the urge to explore was in my blood, for I was born in the Tropics, and though brought home at an early age, I had hazy memories of native life, of warmth and sunshine, of journeys through mysterious forests, and across crocodile-infested rivers. It seemed a long time to wait, but at length school and university days were over and I was really off at last.

I will not weary my reader with a detailed account of my first journey to China, though to me it was a thrilling experience. After a voyage lasting for six weeks I landed at the port of Shanghai in February 1899.[1] The Foreign Settlement in Shanghai, with its magnificent water-front, wide streets, and palatial buildings, is no true reflection of the East. It is only when you leave the foreign quarter and plunge into the native city that you come up against the real thing.

As I approached the city, its temples and pagodas, and its unfamiliar roofscape of coloured tiles, shimmered in the morning light. On its crumbling walls small boys, very quaint in their loose garments and little pigtails, were flying gaudy kites – replicas of birds, fish, dragons, crocodiles. Passing through an ancient gate-way, and down a narrow street, I was in a moment encompassed and hustled along in a

---

1 [FW] Shanghai was one of the first ports in China opened to foreign trade in 1843 as a result of the Opium War. By the end of the nineteenth century there was a long waterfront, 'the Bund', lined with impressive two-storeyed Western buildings with colonnades, and the broad streets of the foreign settlement stretched back from the river. It was not until the first decades of the twentieth century that the huge banks, consulates, hotels and office buildings were built that still line the Bund and create its characteristic skyline.

tumultuous throng. My first bewildered impression was that of having become entangled in the hub of a riot. A feeling approaching panic seized me. Strange faces, many of them hostile and contemptuous, surrounded me, and I soon had a noisy following. The constricted thoroughfares were crowded, and thick with a peculiar odour compounded of spices and stale sweat. Every now and again the shouting of soldiery heralded the approach of a richly caparisoned sedan-chair, carried high on the shoulders of four coolies, and bearing some official personage; usually of great corpulence, and resplendent in his mandarin hat and robes. The escort would shout to the crowd to make way, and anyone slow to comply would be roughly thrust aside. On such occasions it was necessary to flatten oneself against the side to allow the great man and his retinue to pass. There were no pavements on which to take refuge; for the shops, without doors or glass fronts, opened directly on to the streets, which were not more than 10 feet in width. The motley scene, too, was full of colour. Blue predominated in the garments of both men and women; and gold was everywhere in the gilded hieroglyphics inscribed on the vertical shop signs suspended over the heads of the people. The men wore long loose gowns; some of silk, but most of cotton. The sweating coolies were content to be as nature made them, except for a loin-cloth of cotton, and sandals of plaited straw. The women, not many of whom were to be seen, wore very brightly coloured trousers, surmounted by loose tunics. They were evidently contending against great odds in making their way through the turbulent crowd, and their difficulties were greatly increased by the fact that, owing to the pernicious custom of foot-binding, they could only hobble in a stiff, ungainly manner. But I had no opportunity of observing things more closely, for I was myself carried along in the crush; an object of curiosity and derision, and followed by a hooting and jeering mob. Unable to speak a word of the language I could not ask for guidance. How I eventually extricated myself, and found my way back, I cannot recall.

These were some of the impressions received on this my first contact with the Chinese city. Time was to prove that I would spend many

*Ernest Cromwell Peake (right)*
*as a child with one of his brothers.*

years in the interior of the country, where such sights, sounds, and smells would become the commonplace.

A day or two after arrival in Shanghai I boarded one of the big river steamers which trade up the Yang-tse-Kiang, bound for Hankow [Hankou, now part of Wuhan] and beyond.

# Chapter II

# UP THE YANG-TSE-KIANG TO HANKOW

The Yang-tse-Kiang, which interpreted means 'Son of the sea', is the mightiest of the rivers of the Far East. The Chinese also speak of it as the Kin-sah-Kiang, i.e. 'The River of Golden Sand'. Arising high in the snows of the far mountains of Tibet it gathers volume as it flows, until, after a journey of 3000 miles, it pours its waters, laden with yellow sand, into the ocean at Shanghai.

It is difficult at first to realise that one is on a river at all, for the land on either side is lost to sight. Daily, as we proceed upstream, the horizons thicken, until at length the two banks become plainly visible.

As we steamed up against the current, nibbling at the seemingly endless miles, the scene varied considerably. On the northern shore the country, in the main, was low-lying and flat, and largely given over to rice fields; on the southern it was more hilly, but also well cultivated.

There were numerous villages, half-hidden among trees, on the river banks, the inhabitants of which could be seen loitering about, or working in their near-by patches of vegetables. The small wooden houses, roofed with tiles, appeared to be little more than huts promiscuously disposed along the one straggling street. Pigs and chickens moved at will, nosing and picking amidst discarded refuse.

Frequently the close passage of our boat would set all the dogs barking.

On the southern side the hills sometimes reached down to the water's edge. Often the banks were rocky and precipitous, and in such places out-crops of rock would appear through the water, forming little islands very dangerous to navigation. One of these, rising vertically out of the river to a considerable height, and known by the Chinese as 'The Little Orphan', formed a striking feature which could be seen for many miles across the water. The sides of this miniature mountain were covered by a scrubby vegetation, and a Buddhist temple formed the summit. Here and there we would pass a good-sized town nestling in the hollows between the mountains, and around it one could trace the usual massive wall. These battlemented walls were no doubt of value in past times as a protection against enemies, but they are, in these days, of little practical use and are slowly crumbling in decay.

I was surprised at the variety of craft that plied the broad waters of the Yang-tse, from the ocean-going foreign steamer to the smallest native sampan. I noticed at once the preponderance of the flat-bottomed junk, employed so extensively for the transport both of travellers and goods.

We reduced speed repeatedly on our way up river to pick up boat-loads of Chinese passengers. On sighting us from the shore, the large sampans, full of men, women, and children, were rowed swiftly into mid-stream just ahead of the steamer. We slow down. As we overhaul them the native's craft closes in right alongside. Immediately contact is made ropes and grapplers are brought into use to make it fast, and the heavily laden boat, now carried onward apace, is held firmly to the ship's side.

Then follows a most animated and amusing scene, every detail of which I could appreciate from the vantage-point of the upper deck. At a given word the occupants are suddenly galvanised into intense activity. Babies and bundles are heaved on board; their owners scramble after them; and then, in an incredibly short space of time, the sampan is empty and has cast off.

In this manner we picked up hundreds of passengers, and that without a single untoward incident; though I understood that accidents did occasionally happen. Passengers would lose their grip, or miss their footing, fall into the water, and be swept away in an instant. There is no hope of rescue in that powerful current.

For more than 600 miles we forged our way upstream until we reached our destination, the busy trading centre of Hankow. Even at this point, though so far inland, the river is over a mile in width. This will give some impression, perhaps, of the immensity of this great water-way.

Adjoining the vast native city of Hankow, it, in common with the other treaty ports, had its Foreign Settlement. There is a fine river frontage, known as 'The Bund' making an excellent promenade by the water-side. This was the favourite place for the evening stroll, where one might hope for a little breeze and for escape from the ubiquitous mosquito. Well back from the bund were the wide roads and well-built houses of the settlement.

It was in this place that I first met my colleague, Mr A. L. Greig, who had been in China several years before me, and with whom I was to be associated in the distant province of Hunan. As, however, we represented separate spheres of work, I shall, in the following pages, confine myself to my own personal experiences.

I found it necessary to remain some little time in Hankow while I picked up something of the language, and made preparations to continue my journey hundreds of miles further into the interior. A certain amount of furniture was indispensable, and a large stock of provisions had to be accumulated – condensed milk, sugar, tea, flour, and many kinds of tinned goods – as well as a miscellaneous assortment of odds and ends, such as soap, candles, lamps, ironmongery, and tools.

But perhaps the matter which gave me most concern was the engagement of personal servants. I required two men, a 'cook' and a 'boy',[2] the former to confine himself to the daily marketing and to his work in the kitchen; the latter, the more personal attendant, to keeping my rooms in order, making the bed, waiting at table, answering the door, seeing to the comfort of visitors, and so on. He would act as general handy-man, and, if tactful and discriminating, is invaluable as a 'go-between' in dealing with outsiders and callers. The third henchman in a foreign household in China is the 'coolie'. He is engaged for the rough work of the house – windows, floors, shoes, lamps, and water carrying. In the meantime I could dispense with a coolie, but it was

---

2 [ECP] The term 'boy' has no reference to age. It refers to his office. He *may* be a youth, or he may be 40 or 50 years old.

41

important, while I had the opportunity in the big centre of Hankow, to engage the other two.

It was quite extraordinary to me how my arrival had been noted and how my requirements were known even before I knew them myself. I was soon besieged by an army of 'ex-cooks', 'boys' and 'coolies', each protesting his own peculiar fitness and outstanding capacity to undertake the duties required of him. Many of these aspirants to office were rascals who had been employed many times by foreign residents in the Port and been dismissed; but all had a certain amount of training; and all were armed with 'testimonials' extracted from reluctant employers. These letters of recommendation, couched though they frequently were in ambiguous, not to say doubtful, terms, were nevertheless very highly prized by the recipients, who were unable to appreciate the subtleties of expression employed; or even, being written in English, to understand them at all. Quite a brisk trade is carried on in hiring out, or selling these precious documents some of which may even convey veiled warnings to the prospective employer.

As yet I knew next to nothing of the Chinese language and was therefore reduced, while in Hankow, to 'pidgin', or 'business' English, a corrupt lingua franca which has sprung up between natives and foreigners in the Treaty Ports. A good deal of my time was wasted in interviewing quite hopeless applicants, many obviously incompetent; others hard-boiled 'toughs', to all appearances prepared to cut your throat and make off with your possessions at the first convenient opportunity. I was not expert in the use of 'pidgin' English, but conversation would run somewhat as follows:-

I: 'What's your name?'
He: 'Master', (referring to his late employer ) 'he callee me 'Slacker'.
I: 'H'm, that sounds hopeful; what for you leave Master?'
He: 'Master, he catchee one piece wife: Me no likee.'
I: 'What for you no likee lady?'
He: 'Lady, she muchee makee trouble. She talkee me no savvy 'boy-pidgin', no can make bed, no can washee, no can do table all b'long proper. Lady, she no lea'me 'lone all same one piecee man. Master, he

no make trouble. Me do Master two years: Master savvy me b'long good boy.'

I: 'Well, Slacker, s'pose I talkee lady.'

He: (in alarm and seeking desperately, for a way out) 'No can talkee lady! Lady catchee big pain, all same big knife, this side' (indicating vaguely the region of the liver), 'make muchee bad. Doctor, he say, lady no talkee.'

I: 'Ah, that's unfortunate; but now have no time more talkee you. Outside have got one piece boy wantchee talkee me.'

He: 'He no good. He b'long one piece big dam-fool. He no savvy. Me savvy. Me b'long number one, top-side good boy.'

The situation seemed pretty hopeless. But fortune favoured me at last for I was successful in securing the services of a 'cook' and a 'boy' from a British family on the point of returning to England. Chow-ling (the cook) and Ah-shin (the boy) were very highly recommended by their late employers. Chow-ling was of a stocky, powerful build. In disposition he was phlegmatic, 'dour', and inclined to pessimism. But he had 'character', and was reputed to be loyal and reliable. Ah-shin, too, was capable of attachment and constancy, but he was highly-strung and excitable. He was by nature lighter of heart, and more animated; indeed, in every way his temperament was diametrically opposed to that of his colleague. Notwithstanding this contrast the two were very good friends. The testimony of their late employers to their faithful service was fully justified by subsequent experience.

All was now ready for the long journey further inland. I had been entrusted with the task of opening up medical work in the city of Heng-chow, situated in the southern part of the province of Hunan, a tract of country roughly the size of England and Wales. Hunan had the reputation of being the most conservative and the most bitterly anti-foreign province in China. At the time of which I speak foreigners had not been able to take up permanent residence there. The few who had ventured to travel in that region had been roughly handled and hounded out. I had before me a journey of some 400 miles by native boat; for at Hankow it was necessary to bid farewell to all means of modern travel; and indeed to all touch with Western civilisation. Progress would be slow. It had taken seven weeks to reach Hankow from London. I was now warned that it might take as long again to my destination. In that case, as regards time, I was but half-way to the end of my travels. But that did not worry me. There was no occasion to hurry, and long leisurely progress would give opportunity to contemplate the country and the people. I was about to sample a cross-section of pure China – untouched by the foreign influences that are so manifest at the open ports.[3] Although this appealed to me I knew of course, that the enterprise was full of peril.

For the first 130 miles I was to push up the Yang-tse, and then to follow one of its main tributaries for another 200 odd miles until we reached Heng-chow (or Heng-yang as it now called) situated on the banks of the river. As there were many junks moored against the river-bank at Hankow I sent Ah-shin off to secure one of them for the complete journey. He appeared much gratified to be entrusted with such a responsible task, and spent the day boarding one boat after another, investigating its condition and accommodation, and bargaining over the terms of hire. He returned triumphant in the evening, having succeeded in chartering a good, commodious house-boat, complete with skipper and crew, free of cargo, comparatively clean, and at a

---

3 [FW] The first ports in China to be opened to foreign trade were mainly coastal. The treaty of Tientsin (1858) at the end of the Second Opium War included the upriver, inland port of Hankou (Hankow) in Hunan Province, which is now part of the triple city of Wuhan (comprising Hanyang, Wuchang and Hankou at the confluence of the Han and Yang-tse rivers). Foreigners were technically restricted to their concessions in the treaty ports and not allowed to travel further inland without permission, a prohibition that was ignored by many missionaries. The Treaty of Tientsin did include a stipulation allowing missionaries to travel more freely, but this was not easy. Griffith John (1831–1912) of the London Missionary Society arrived in China in 1855 and spent his life working in Hunan and Hubei provinces, but always from his base in the city. Whether Hunan was more anti-foreign than other inland provinces is not certain, but any missionaries travelling inland were likely to encounter hostility, both from local officials aware of the illegality of their movements and from the local population. After decades of sporadic anti-foreign events, when Dr Peake arrived in China, the last years of the nineteenth century saw the rise of the Boxer movement, originally an anti-Manchu uprising in Shandong (Shantung) and north China which gradually turned against foreign institutions like the railways, and which culminated in the Siege of the Legations in Peking in 1900.

44

reasonable figure. I went down to have a look at the boat and was pleased with her. In common with her type she was built high in the stern to provide room for the skipper, who is in charge of the tiller. In contrast to the stern the bows were low and square and, in order that the boat might clearly see its way, were embellished with large eyes painted in vivid colours on the wood-work. She had large brown sails, reinforced by bamboo struts, and was reported to be capable of travelling at a high speed with a following wind.

The next day was spent in loading up the vessel with my personal belongings and the numerous cases of stores, and as we intended to make an early start the following morning if the wind was favourable, we spent the night on board.

Ah-shin had fixed me up very comfortably in the compartment which was to be my bed-room. To one side was my sleeping-berth. There was a broad bunk on the other side also which served admirably for one's clothes and wash-basin. From this compartment a door opened into a small space towards the stern, next to the skipper's quarters, and another door opened forward into the living section. This latter was furnished with a small dining table and chairs. From here, by ascending a couple of steps and passing through a small side-door, one was able to get out on to the long narrow foot-way which extended along the whole length of the boat. This cat-walk, raised about two feet above the surface of the water, formed the usual means of communication from one part of the junk to another, there being side-doors in most of the compartments. Forward from the living-room were the galley and boys' quarters, and next to them there was accommodation for the crew of four. The deck-house stopped well short of the bows, leaving an open space in the prow – a great boon in fine weather.

I was awakened at dawn, that first morning, by shouts from the lao-pan,[4] the movements of the crew, and the hauling up of the anchor. There was much cackling, of the fowls brought on board as part provision for the journey. Putting my head through the little window at my bedside I felt a light breeze from an easterly direction and knew

---

4 [ECP] lao-pan – the skipper (literally the 'old plank')

45

that we would soon be off. With a rhythmic 'oh-ya, oh-ya' they were hoisting the sail to the mast-head; and when I looked out again I found that, in spite of the powerful current against us, we were slowly moving upstream.

It was not long before a bend in the river shut Hankow completely from our view, and I felt that I had indeed cut myself adrift from my friends and security. What lay before me I could not tell. A sense of profound loneliness came over me. But there could be no turning back.

**Chapter III**

# BY HOUSE-BOAT TO HENG-CHOW

The first day, with a fair wind, we made good progress. The skipper, a good-natured elderly man, was in good humour. Evidently the gods were propitious, and his luck was in. He would burn a stick or two of incense to conciliate the spirits and ensure a continuance of their favours.

But the gods were not always willing to co-operate. There were times when for days we would be completely stuck, the wind being adverse, and the current being too strong. On such occasions there was nothing for it but to tie-up under the high bank and await better conditions. The boat was comfortable and weather-proof, and it was not difficult to take such delays philosophically.

These stoppages, moreover, gave me the opportunity of taking walks along the river-side, and making abortive attempts at conversation with workers in the paddy-fields. I had so far acquired but few phrases, such as the customary greeting 'Chee-lias-fan-pa?' (Have you had your rice), and 'Kwei-hsing?' (What is your honourable name); and was gratified to find myself understood. Intercourse, however, with such meagre conversational exchange, could not long be sustained, and was, with mutual smiles and bows, soon concluded.

When the wind dropped, an attempt would often be made to push on by means of 'tracking'. Three or four of the crew would go ashore and haul the junk along by means of a bamboo rope attached to the mast-head. If the river banks were low and muddy, or rocky, or otherwise unsuitable for tracking, recourse would be had, in shallow water, to 'poling'. The four men would each take a long pole, then starting from the bows but facing towards the stern, would plunge their poles to the bottom, press their shoulders to the free end, and bending to their work, would slowly force their way to the stern by walking along the outer cat-walks, thus pushing the boat along from under their feet. Arrived at the stern they would pull up their poles, walk smartly back to the bows, and repeat the process. This major 'punting', necessitating the expenditure of much strength and energy, would sometimes go on with monotonous regularity for a whole morning. There were occasions when neither sailing, nor tracking, nor poling was possible, and then we might have to fall back on 'sculling'. For this, two long and powerful sculls are used, each worked by two men standing at the bows and manipulating the massive oar with a side-to-side action. Sculling frequently came in very useful in deep water, as when it was necessary to cross from one side of the river to the other. It will be seen from this that, except when we had a good wind, progress was slow. The days were warm, the nights pleasantly cool. Life, for the time being, had become one long day-dream.

There was always much to see. Occasionally we passed through a big city, throbbing with life; and sometimes by a busy little town, with its houses crowded right down to the water's edge. Then, just outside the town, to bring good luck to the neighbourhood, would come the inevitable pagoda.

We slipped by numerous villages, where life appeared very peaceful and unhurried; the women washing clothes at the river's brink, or loitering about with the children, the men working in their patches of vegetables, or fishing close in-shore. One morning I had quite a near view of the native method of fishing. A large net, spread out and supported by a bamboo frame-work, was lowered from the bows of the sampan. The rower, standing in the stern, was, by a backward stroke, propelling the boat slowly and noiselessly against the stream, and in this way scooping up whatever fish might come within range. Periodically he would raise the net and remove the catch by means of another small net mounted on a long handle. In this leisurely way he was securing quite a big haul.

It must have been about the tenth day that we turned south from the Yang-tse and pushed out way against a strong current into the estuary of the Siang [Xiang]; the tributary which I was to ascend and which flows through the province of Hunan. Soon the water began to get wider and wider. We kept close in to the eastern bank, but it was not long before the opposite shore was out of sight. My map showed that we had entered the Tung-ting [Dongting] lake, a sheet of water having an area equal to that of an average-sized English county. Evidently the river widened into this great expanse shortly before it emptied itself into the main stream. Junks and fishing craft were sailing across the broad waters; but, for ourselves, we hugged the bank and edged our way along by poling or tracking. Had there been a helpful breeze we might have attempted short cuts across the little bays and inlets, but the lake had an evil reputation for sudden and violent storms, involving much wreckage and loss of life, and our 'old plank' was not inclined to take risks. His caution was well justified, for soon after entering the lake a boisterous wind swept down from the hills, lashing the placid waters into a turbulent sea. We managed to manoeuvre into the shelter of a friendly creek and tied up. There we were, in calm water and security, while the storm raged without.

I comforted myself with the reflection that such an abrupt gale could not last, and that we would soon be on our way again. In this I was mistaken. Day after day the wind screamed over our rigging, and to make any move was out of the question. But, apart from the delay, we suffered no great inconvenience. We were in a safe haven, and there was plenty of food on board. My own stores provided for all my needs, and the crew were well supplied with rice. Moreover Chow-ling was able to make several excursions ashore, visiting native huts and purchasing chickens and eggs.

The wind abated as suddenly as it had arisen, after raging for well over a week, and we were able to push on once more. We had made a fortunate escape; but much wreckage, both floating and tossed ashore, gave evidence of the disaster which had overtaken many others.

As the storm had now fallen to a dead calm we were forced to track along the edge of the lake for days, until one morning the far shore again became visible, and resolved itself at length into the river bank of the opposite side. We were out of the lake at last. The lao-pan and his crew were obviously pleased. The gods had continued to show their good-will. Clearly it was an occasion to be suitably celebrated. That evening, when we had come to anchor, and in the calm hush and stillness of sunset, a live fowl was brought forward from the hen-roost. Incense sticks were solemnly lighted and erected on the bows. The men, standing in a semi-circle and led by 'the old man' in a high-pitched voice intoned mystical incantations while one of the crew, armed with a large vegetable knife, cut the throat of the inoffensive bird, allowing the blood to flow over the side of the boat into the water – a thanks-offering to the protesting spirits.

In the still weather succeeding the storm I was able to take many a stroll ashore and to pass through many small river-side villages. Through these would pass the main straggling road-way with wooden or mud dwellings clustered about it, and in which live-stock roamed at will and children tumbled over each other in their play. The adult population would be engaged in their various occupations, but one and all would stop to stare at the outlandish foreigner who had suddenly made his appearance in midst. Never before had any of them seen a 'Western barbarian'. But from these simple country people I met with no rudeness. After the first gasp of astonishment they would smile and bow and call off the barking dogs. Invariably I found the people in the villages much more friendly than those in the towns and cities. As a rule the men were busy in the rice fields, irrigating their plots by the use of ingenious devices for drawing water up from the river, or ploughing the land, the primitive wooden plough being drawn by the fearsome water-buffalo.[5]

---

5 [ECP] This powerful brute which is armed with formidable horns is most amenable to its master, and even to his small children, but savage and dangerous to the stranger. I never myself had any unpleasant experiences with the water-buffalo, but I heard of a foreigner having a very narrow escape from one of these animals. The brute charged and he had to run for his life, but succeeded in reaching, and clambering up a tree. There he had to remain all night, for the beast, though foiled, waited for his quarry below and declined to vacate his post. Relief came in the early morning in the shape of a very small boy. For him behemoth obediently lowered his huge head. The child stepped upon it, lightly sprang upon his back, and rode off!

50

The women also had their outside duties, the chief of which appeared to be their responsibility for the domestic washing. Long rows could frequently be seen kneeling side by side at the water's edge rinsing and wringing out the family garments; the whole process accompanied, needless to say, by much chatter.

One evening, emerging from a small hamlet, I had to negotiate a creek which ran inland for a short distance. The sun was setting behind the hills on the far side of the river, giving a glow of colour to the scene. In the foreground was a fisherman standing in his flat-bottomed sampan, which floated like a petal on the surface of the water. He was naked, except for his cotton loin-cloth and wide-brimmed hat. As he stood poised there in the stern with a bamboo pole in his hand his inverted reflection in the water reproduced every detail. Some large birds were sitting in the boat, and others were swimming and diving round about it. Presently one bobbed up from the depths with a shining fish in its beak, and I then realised that I was watching the native method of fishing with cormorants. Rings around the birds' necks prevented them from swallowing their catch. On rising to the surface the fisherman brought them aboard by the use of the long pole, the end of which he thrust into the water under their feet. The bird was then brought into the boat, relieved of its prey, and thrown back on the water. In this way he was kept busy tossing fish after fish to the bottom of the sampan now glistening with his spoils. So absorbed was he in his task that he had not noticed me standing on the bank, but when at length he glanced my way his eyes and mouth opened wide with amazement. So I called out the familiar and friendly salutation 'Have you had your rice?' This seemed to put him more at his ease, and he replied with a polite bow. When I gave him a farewell wave of the hand his look of surprise had been replaced by a wide grin. He'd have something to tell them when he got home that night!

As I drew nearer to my journey's end I conceived the idea of making a more extensive excursion ashore. This would relieve the monotony of the long boat trip and make a welcome break. The distance had seemed interminable. Day after day the cold, clear water swished endlessly past the sides of our junk. Morning after morning the horizon was just as distant. What a relief it would be to have a really good spell ashore! I had heard of the sacred mountain of the South known as the Nan-yoh-san, and I knew it was within easy distance of the town of Heng-shan which we would pass. Why not make an exploratory detour of the mountain?[6]

Accordingly, soon after arrival at Heng-shan, accompanied by both Chow-ling and Ah-shin, I went ashore, leaving boat and possessions in the charge of our honest old lao-pan. Ah-shin very quickly collected the coolies we required for the baggage – bedding and provisions – as I expected to be away at least one night. Unfortunately the local magistrate had been informed of the arrival of a foreigner, and fearing there might be a disturbance he sent two mounted officers and a guard of twelve soldiers to protect me, together with a sedan-chair and bearers. They met us not far from the water front. There was no help for it but to accept the escort; so after polite formalities we lined up into quite an imposing little cavalcade and started off, causing a decided sensation as we passed through the streets of the little town. The place had a lively air. Dogs and livestock were everywhere mixing freely with the populace. A woman chasing chickens out of her little shop was suddenly petrified, and the townsfolk going about their morning shopping were brought to an abrupt stand-still, as they caught sight of me. However, we were not molested, and were soon out on the open plain – lovely with the fresh greenness of the young rice.

On reaching the foot-hills we left the chair and the ponies behind, and soon began the ascent of the holy mountain itself. All the way up there is a granite-paved track forming a gigantic staircase, the stones of which have been worn down by the feet of pilgrims for 1,000 years. Wayside shrines and temples are located at frequent intervals all the way to the summit. I was informed that every year, in the eighth month, tens of thousands of pilgrims arrive, many from far distant places, to worship the idols on the sacred mount. The long line of devotees would toil up in single file, prostrating themselves as they went, halting at each shrine

---

6 [FW] Nanyue shan or Heng shan, Hunan, one of the Five Sacred Mountains of China, places of imperial pilgrimage for centuries, not to be confused with the Four Buddhist Mountains.

to burn incense and to make supplication before the gilded image of the Buddha – it may be for the recovery of a sick one at home, or that a son might be born to the family.

There were not many pilgrims at the time that I made my trip up the mountain, so I had ample opportunity to inspect the temples. I found them invariably dark, damp, and dirty. The floors were of brick or beaten earth, the tiled roofs were leaky, the walls filthy, the windows usually of tattered paper, and the whole place rife with vermin.

It was pretty late when we reached the summit, where the biggest and most sacred of the temples was situated. It had a strikingly ornate roof and glazed yellow tiles, the corners of the eaves being pointed and tilted upwards. The roof ridges were crowded with the grotesque images of many different creatures – dragons, lions, and dogs – in order that no vacant space be left upon which a malicious Devil might perch himself. The roof was supported by massive wooden pillars, heavily lacquered and very handsome. Pavilions, overhung by high trees, flanked the temple building on each side; and on the terrace was an enormous bronze brazier in which incense was kept perpetually burning.

Passing through the main portico one entered the lofty central hall and was immediately confronted by a colossal figure of the benign Buddha, sitting cross-legged upon his lotus throne, and lost in unending contemplation. Here is the grand climax, the sanctum sanctorum, and here, before the great graven image, the pilgrims make their final prostrations, while the shaven priests, in their long grey robes, walk in slow procession around the worshippers.

I was courteously received by the old Abbot, who generously offered me for the night the use of his own room, an apartment opening off the central hall. By the use of my oiled ground-sheet laid on the rickety bed, insect powder, and mosquito-net, I passed a fair night; disturbed only by the periodic beating of the bronze gong, the fitful tom-tom of the ox-hide drum, and the weird chanting of the priests.

I was up early in the morning and glad to get out into the fresh mountain air. It had been too dark to see the view at the time of our arrival, but now, standing 4,000 feet above the plain, I beheld range upon range of clear-cut mountains on the sky-line, temples and pagodas on the near foot-hills, and in the mid-distance, lakes and villages in the midst of vast rice fields which showed us great splashes of vivid green. And there, winding its course across the plain, was the river we had so recently left behind us.

In the immediate vicinity of the temple were some gigantic pine trees, regarded by the priests as most sacred. Under one of these was a great flat rock with a shallow depression on its upper surface, the shape of which suggested the impress of an immense human foot. The impression was, as I remember it, some five feet in length. I was unable to follow much of the legend with regard to this 'foot-print', as told me by the Abbot, but I did understand that it was where the god of the temple landed when he alighted from the heavens.

I felt much tempted to remain a day or two at this lovely place. But, unfortunately, Ah-shin had prepared my breakfast inside, and as I entered the recess in which he had set the table I was staggered by the most disgusting stench. I soon discovered that the nauseating odour emanated from a flat crawling insect, shaped like a shield, and from half to three quarters of an inch in length, which literally covered the walls and window frames. I was so sickened by the smell that the very thought of breakfast was revolting. I hurried out of the place telling Ah-shin to pack up, and that we would leave without delay. He obeyed reluctantly, and was so concerned by my declining to eat that he too refused to take his rice! Not so Chow-ling, who made the best of his opportunity, and disposed of several bowls of rice, together with vegetables and chunks of pork.

The climb up the mountain-side had been a hard toilsome grind; the stone steps being set so high above each other. There had been much groaning and cursing among the escort. Indeed, at one point, they had seemed to be on the verge of rioting, declaring they could go no further, and demanding to put up for the night at a temple about three quarters of the way up. The trouble had been surmounted by the promise of a little 'wine-money'. All were in much better spirits, however, after the night's rest at the top. The descent down the mountain was made at a rapid pace and in great good humour.

On arrival back at the boat, the wind being northerly, we immediately set sail. I was conscious now of an inward thrill, for I knew that, barring accidents, I was within a day or two of my destination. The weather held good, and on the afternoon of the second day we reached our objective, the goal of many weeks of strange travel, the archaic city of Heng-chow.

# Chapter IV

# EARLY DAYS

Travelling through the Provinces, and keeping mainly to the boat, I had not so far encountered the hostility of the people. I suppose that not one in a thousand of the inhabitants of Hunan had ever seen a 'Western barbarian'.[7] But it was widely known, and universally accepted, that the 'foreign devil' was indeed a devil. This I was made to feel immediately I set foot on the stone steps leading up from the river-side at our evil smelling landing place.

Descending from the boat I very nearly lost my balance on the smooth stones, rendered slippery by scum and refuse. My debut was in consequence rather unfortunate, and, I fear, suffered some loss of dignity. I was conscious of a gasp of astonishment at my arrival. It was only a matter of seconds before we were surrounded by a most curious crowd, gaping in undisguised wonderment at the uncivilised boar from beyond the seas.

Amazement, at first, held the crowd speechless, as they pushed forward to see over and past one another. Adroitly seizing his opportunity before signs of rowdiness should manifest themselves, Chow-ling – who with Ah-shin and two of the boatmen had accompanied me ashore as personal body-guard – attempted to humour the people by addressing them in courteous terms. He was a man of few words, and could be a tough customer on occasion; but he did not go about looking

---

7 [FW] Though any Hunanese who had visited Hankou might have seen foreigners, it is almost certain that no-one in Hengyang would have had such a chance and their distinctive appearance and different clothing marked Europeans out. The first Dutch visitors in the South were known as 'red hairs' but the epithet *yang guizi*, 'foreign devil', was also applied.

for trouble. 'Let us pass, good people', he said. 'We are unworthy to set foot in your honourable city, but at least we come to you as friends, and have only good-will in our hearts. Open a way and permit us to pass, and may you have peace'.

I could gather that such was the tenor of his words, and hoped they might be effective. We pressed forward, and as we did so the crowd fell back on each side. So far there had been, for the most part, silence and stupefaction. But soon insulting remarks and derisive shouts arose from some of those in the rear. 'He's a spy', 'Throw him out', 'Sah yang Kiwei-tsz'(i.e. Kill the foreign devil). The contagion spread. In an incredibly short space of time the attitude of the mob changed from one of inquisitive curiosity into one of ugly and aggressive animosity. Lumps of dirt, fortunately ill-aimed, began to fly around from those on the outer ring. All the time we continued to press forward, led by one of the boatmen, who was conducting us to a river-side inn. We reached this in safety, the doors were closed and bolted after us, and the crowd, after a noisy demonstration in the street, finally dispersed.

I was forced to remain for many months in my poor native quarters – subsisting mainly on chicken, eggs, and rice – before finally acquiring more suitable premises of my own. During this time I had to be careful to show myself as little as possible. To venture out upon the street would instantly attract a disorderly throng. The more hostile would shout, 'Ya, foreign devil, beat him!'; the less ill-disposed would press around excitedly, scrutinise me from head to foot, feel my clothes, and ask innumerable questions. They would make remarks on the colour of my hair and eyes. Blue eyes amazed them. 'Cat's eyes', they shouted, 'and no pigtail, and look at his outlandish clothes!' It was impossible to go far, or to do much on my own account, eager as I was to explore the streets and shops, and to observe the people and their strange ways in this strange city.

As it was necessary for me to get about in order to inspect the different properties which were for sale, I purchased my own sedan-chair. To hire chair-bearers was an easy matter when ever one wished to venture out. Fully enclosed within this, and having a latticed curtain which could be let down in front, I was able to see without being observed myself. In this way I acquired a good idea of the geography of the city, and of its wide extent. The narrow tortuous streets seemed always to be over-crowded. They were paved with stone: and on both sides of the road there were open sewers, the offensive odour permeating the stagnant atmosphere. The houses were of 'jerry 'construction, built of timber and brick, with tiled roofs. Shops, with open fronts, lined the thoroughfares just beyond the noisome drains; a paving stone functioning as a bridge for the customers.

The shops contained goods of all descriptions – basket-ware, crockery, a multiplicity of articles made from bamboo, wooden buckets, clothing materials, and so on. Some of the larger shops were stocked with a very fine assortment of beautifully coloured silks of high quality. These latter were much frequented by the local gentry, who rode in their chairs or sauntered leisurely down the streets, in sharp contrast to the humble coolies actively engaged in their various tasks.

I was struck by the large number of street-hawkers, and by the varieties of the wares which they carry suspended from the extremities of their bamboo poles. There were baskets, brushes, bundles of firewood, paper lanterns, palm-leaf fans, live fish and eels in tubs, gold-fish, vegetables, melons and dates, edible bamboo shoots and lotus lily seeds, peanuts, sweets and cakes, eggs, and even water, for sale.

Then seated at the road-side, there were letter-writers for the illiterate (which comprises the vast majority of the population); story-tellers; puppet-shows; barbers shaving heads; and travelling cooks, cooking tasty bits on their portable stoves, with semi-naked children and mangy dogs sniffing around.

At night I found there was no street lighting. Each pedestrian carries his own ornate paper lantern. If out in your chair after dark your servant carries the lantern just ahead of the bearers, who shout to clear their path; the people fall back, the dogs snarl and slink aside, and you pass on.

My quarters at the inn were cramped, dark, and inconvenient. There was no glass in the place, the windows being filled in with greased paper. The floors were of mud. There was no ceiling over one's head, only the bare tiles, loose and leaky. The rain dripped through in a dozen places. My two rooms were bare and comfortless, and my servants' quarters even more so.

The street was very noisy, both day and night. In the day-time there were strident cries of the street-hawkers, beating their gongs and proclaiming their wares; the shouts of the chair-bearers to clear the way; the vociferous quarrels of the women, in high-pitched voices calling down the curses of the gods upon their opponents; the creaking and squeaking of the heavily-laden wheelbarrow; and many other extraneous noises of a nerve-racking character.

At night my sleep was disturbed by the letting-off of fire-crackers, and beating of gongs, to scare away malignant spirits; and by the barking of the half-wild native dog, a savage wolf-like creature that seemed to have a special predilection for the legs of beggars and foreigners.

There were other sleep-destroying noises. Periodically, perhaps every hour or so, the night watchman, coming down the empty street on his customary beat, would strike his gong with great vigour, making the whole neighbourhood resound with its metallic reverberations. The object of this night-patrol is, ostensibly, to strike terror into all ruffians, thieves, and bad characters who may be lurking in the vicinity, and warn them to make off while the going is good. Needless to say the effect of this farcical procedure is absolutely nil so far as the black-legs are concerned. They know that a scuffle with burglars is the last thing that the watchman desires. His object is not to *catch* the thief, but to give him notice of his approach. Let the evil-doer be sensible then, and lie low until he has passed!

That I found to be the usual routine as regards night patrol of the streets. Now and again, when the Chief Magistrate exhibited a flash of determination to round up the marauders, he would detach several of the braves to accompany the watchman, and then some sort of show would be made to effect arrests. But that was a small matter. All that was necessary was for the leader of the robbers to come to terms with the corporal. When the latter had been satisfactorily 'squared' all was well, and the gang was free to proceed unhindered.

Further acquaintance with life in the Celestial Empire was to prove that blackmail, bribery, and corruption permeated the whole social structure from top to bottom; from the Empress-Dowager and her notoriously rapacious eunuchs, and from the highest officials, down to the meanest underlings and parasites.

But to return to the noises which, in those early days, so often disturbed my slumbers and rendered the nights hideous. In addition to such as I have mentioned, I was much mystified by voices calling and halloo-ing as they passed down the deserted street. At first they would be faint and far away, but grew louder and more distinct as they approached, until at last the very words could be distinguished. These words resolved themselves into a wailing appeal for the return of a departing spirit. Someone, it might be a child, lay dying at home. The spirit was leaving, or had just vacated, the body. Perhaps it might even yet, while still in the vicinity of the home, be induced to return. So one or two adult members of the family must set out to call back the wanderer. In order to strengthen the appeal, garments and other once-cherished possessions were carried and waved in the air. 'Come back, come back', the voices cry; 'Here is your little embroidered coat, and the coloured sash that you loved so much. Don't you recognise them? Your parents weep and beg you to come home'.

Sleep was made difficult, too, for other reasons. Very often the temperature, which had been round about 90°F during the day, would be much the same at night, the mercury falling but little. And a dead, moist heat at that. One longed for a breeze, or at least some little movement of the air, but this was impossible – apart from the constant use of one's fan – shut in as we were, and surrounded by high walls.

The bodily discomfort due to the heat and atmospheric stagnation was further accentuated by the myriads of torturing mosquitoes. This made the use of a net imperative. I had often cause to bless my net as I lay, bathed in perspiration, inside it, and could hear the ravenous creatures buzzing outside – furious at being baulked of their prey. There was also 'the pestilence that walketh in darkness' that no net could exclude.

Even on the hottest nights I was, for the sake of privacy, confined to my sordid apartment. Not so the other inmates of the house, who would take their sleeping mats into the open courtyard, and would lie there fanning themselves far into the night. Indeed, many of the city's inhabitants, on these sweltering summer nights, would carry their simple bamboo couches out into the malodorous street in order to catch any little passing breeze.

And there were the rats! Under cover of darkness they would come out in battalions. The scrambling and scampering of these creatures, their gnawing of one's shoes, or nibbling at the bedside candle, were sufficient in themselves to destroy all hope of repose.

But occasionally there were other visitors even less to be desired – night robbers! I was visited several times. Early one morning Ah-shin burst into my room shouting 'Thieves, thieves!' and immediately bolted out again. Awakened out of a deep sleep I felt dazed and stupid. More than that I felt 'doped'. Nevertheless I rose and staggered after him, in my pyjamas, with a confused idea of helping Ah-shin to seize hold of the intruders. I found him again when I reached the courtyard, which was surrounded by a high mud wall. 'Where are they, Ah-shin?' I said in a stage whisper. 'Gone!' he exclaimed, flinging out both arms in his most dramatic manner. 'They must have gone hours ago. Look, Sir, that's where they got in'. I looked in the direction in which he pointed, and there, in the early morning light, I discovered a hole, big enough for the passage of a man's body, low down in the wall. Unable to climb the wall the thieves had dug through it. Lying near was a stout iron cabin trunk which had been taken from the foot of my bed, and which had proved too big to pass through the hole. The box was heavy and probably thought to contain silver. They had failed to force the lock, and finding they could not pass it through the wall, probably also being pressed for time, had abandoned it.

By this time the land-lord and all the inmates were thoroughly aroused and had congregated in the central court. Ah-shin, still in a highly excitable condition, went from one to another volubly explaining how, having occasion to rise early and go into the rear court, he had discovered the doctor's iron trunk, and near it the hole in the wall. Chow-ling was the last to make his tardy appearance. He was as imperturbable as ever, and seemed to regard Ah-shin's loquacity with a mild contempt. 'Good Sir' he said at last, addressing the land-lord, 'let us have our rice, and afterwards we can report this matter to the Magistrate'.

I returned to my room to investigate. My medicine-chest which the robbers had probably mistaken for a cash-box, had gone; and also my much-valued small travelling clock. My watch fortunately had escaped for it had been under my pillow. Clothing was scattered about the floor; foreign dress would have been useless. But a number of small articles had disappeared from the pockets, and the braces removed from my trousers. Gone also were brush and comb, candlestick and soap-dish. The heavy trunk would require two men to remove it. Moreover they must have had a light, for without it the room would have been in complete darkness. With all this going on, how was it that I, a light sleeper, did not wake? In accordance with their practice a soft light would be furnished by the glow of a burning incense stick, the fumes from which are also strongly narcotic. The plan is to hold the stick close to the sleeper's face; as the smoke is inhaled his slumbers become more and more profound. No wonder I felt doped. But perhaps it was just as well that I did not wake. Such men are resolute and carry daggers, which, if tackled, they do not hesitate to use.

As time went on, discomforts and inconveniences only increased and my health began to suffer. Privacy, my most pressing need, was almost impossible, and the question of finding suitable premises of my own became an urgent one. This took some time, but ultimately I was offered a property which turned out to be most suitable. It had been on the market for a long time, but no buyer could be found as the place had the reputation of being 'haunted'. It was situated at the southern end of the city, close to the river, and occupied about one and a half acres of ground. A high brick wall surrounded it, the front opening directly on to the street.

Just within the solid wooden gateway was a courtyard, with the gate-keeper's lodge to one side. On both sides of the enclosure were pavilions in the native style, with paper windows set in ornate wood-work, and tiled roofs with tilted eaves. With certain adaptation I could see that these rooms would serve admirably for commencing medical work. There was accommodation for a waiting room, consulting room, dispensary, a ward for a few beds with adjoining kitchen, and nearby a small detached place which could be furnished with glass windows and converted into an operating room. There were other small apartments which would come in very useful for hospital assistants.

The rear of this enclosure was bounded by a colour-washed brick wall surmounted by ornamental tiles. In this wall was a great circular opening through which one passed into a still more spacious area. Here again were good living quarters, more solidly built, and of more picturesque architecture than in the forecourt.

The central portion was laid out as a garden. There was an artificial pond for lotus lilies and goldfish, and round about were fruit trees – orange, banana and fig. There was one large tree, which especially interested me. It was obviously of the citrus family; for the fruit, which glowed like big spheres of gold among the dark green leaves, resembled enormous grape-fruit nearly the size of a human head. This was my first acquaintance with the pomelo.

This same enclosure, with its private living rooms and garden, was just what I required. The place was well back from the street and therefore quiet, and the high wall of solid brick, which surrounded the whole property gave efficient protection against robbers. In the simple one-floor buildings in the rear of the area there was ample accommodation for all my needs – bedroom, dining room study, guest-room, as well as kitchen quarters, and rooms for my two men. The latter were enthusiastic at the prospect of moving to this new place, and having a home of our own. Ah-shin, hardly able to contain himself in his excitement, seemed to forget his ordinary duties. Chow-ling, on the other hand, working in the miserable inn 'kitchen' stolidly continued with his marketing and cooking. No impending changes, however thrilling, could distract him from his constant faithful service.

Inwardly I, too, was excited. In the fore-court opening on to the street, the buildings were, as I have said, suitable and adaptable for the opening up of medical work; and in the living quarters, behind they required little more to make them habitable than to be appropriately furnished. It was very necessary, however, that in our business negotiations with the owner we should preserve an inscrutable exterior. To have betrayed our feelings by showing too great an interest in the place, or to have evinced keenness to acquire it, would have sent the price soaring sky-high; and perhaps a very long waiting period, before we could have come to anything like reasonable terms.

The Chinese are adept in the art of bargaining. No transaction in buying and selling is satisfactory without preliminary chaffer. The vendor, in the first place, puts his figure many times higher than the actual value, and acts as if, in doing so, he is positively giving it away. The purchaser is, of course, appropriately shocked. He turns to leave in disgust, but as he does so will throw out an offer much below the sum that he is in reality willing to pay. This is treated with scorn, but a lower figure is shouted after the retreating customer, who may now be half-way down the street. The latter is thus induced to return and the comedy continues. These contests are much enjoyed by the participants, and also by the by-standers. Life is leisurely, time is of no consideration, and, in important deals, a wordy war may be protracted off and on for many days, weeks, or even months. The seller, little by little, lowers his figure; the purchaser very gradually raises his, ultimately a price is fixed, and this is frequently about mid-way between the two extremes. With regard to the property which I was so anxious to acquire, thanks to the fact that the place was said to be haunted by disembodied spirits, possession, at a reasonable cost, was not long delayed.

It was a great day when I was able to leave the native inn and transfer myself and my belongings to the new home. My two men threw themselves into the work of removal with avidity. Ah-shin could now freely express his delight, and Chow-ling growled his satisfaction. The settling down process began at once, and life assumed a very different complexion. At last I was able to command complete privacy. The publicity of the inn had become well-nigh intolerable. But the quiet and seclusion of my new quarters brought intense relief. I was able now to unpack in peace the many cases I had brought up-country with me, and was gratified to find so little damage to my possessions. Even the crockery had, in the main, arrived whole. Shelves were soon fixed up in my study-sitting room by a local carpenter, and it was good to see my books again ranged around the walls. I felt that I had now secured a foot-hold in the place. I could lean back, and take stock of my position, prepared for whatever the future might unfold.

# Chapter V

# DIGGING IN

Soon after settling down I realised the importance of engaging a gate-keeper and a coolie. Any visitor would of necessity have to hammer on the street gate. In the rear court this would not be heard. It was in accordance with custom to have a gate-keeper in his lodge next to the street. His duty was to attend to all callers, and report matters to Ah-shin, who in turn would inform me. Visitors, such as officials paying ceremonial calls, could be brought right though to my K'eh-fang, or guest-room. Patients, if such were to come, would be shown into the out-patient waiting-room.

With the help of my friend the inn-keeper I was enabled to secure both gate-man and coolie without much delay. For the rough work, and particularly as water-carrier, the latter was urgently required. He turned out a satisfactory servant. But not so the former, who, I discovered later, was a confirmed opium habitué. He was found to be constantly away from the gate-house. Later it transpired that he frequented an opium den a little way down the street. One night, finding that he was not at home, I was guided to the cellar myself. Stooping through a low doorway, and descending a few steps, I found myself in a veritable dungeon. It was dimly lighted by a number of tiny lamps, one by the side of each rough bedstead. The heavy narcotising odour of opium fumes pervaded the place, which was full to capacity; each man lying on his side and smoking the lethal drug. They had yellow, mask-like faces, and clouded eyes.

An attendant was going from bench to bench serving out the raw drug. A little of the viscous stuff was taken up by the smoker on a slender stilette and twisted round in the flame of the small lamp. It was then transferred to the bowl of the long pipe, which was again heated, while the fumes inhaled. One man was hiding his face, obviously with the idea of escaping detection. I turned him over, and discovered my gate-keeper. As I walked out he rose and very sheepishly followed me. But to keep a hopeless debauchee of his type was out of the question. I was, however, more fortunate in his successor who proved a steady and reliable servant in the difficult days to come.

One of my early problems in Heng-chow was concerned with the question of water supply. The city derived its water from the river and from wells. The latter were very numerous, in some areas practically every house had its own well. If the boring and blasting was carried through a rocky stratum some twenty or thirty feet deep a good pure water was obtained. But it was very liable to become infected from surface contamination. River water was always heavily polluted; and it was on the river that I was at first obliged to depend. Later on I had a well dug in my own garden with very satisfactory results. It served also as a cool chamber for the preservation of food which would otherwise perish in the heat. It was our refrigerator, the food being lowered in a suitable receptacle to just above the water level. Around the well I planted banana trees which grew up with wonderful rapidity, their great leaves affording grateful shade from the tropical sun.

It was a great relief when the work of digging the well was completed, not only because of the great convenience of having our own water right on the spot, but also because there were times when it was of great importance to be independent of an outside supply, particularly when there was unrest abroad, and when anti-foreign feeling was running high. These outbreaks of hostility were liable to recur periodically, especially in times of distress, as from drought, epidemic, or flood. On such occasions it would certainly be rumoured that the foreigner was at the bottom of it all. Undoubtedly, by his fiendish arts, he had vitiated the feng-shui or 'luck' of the city, and was responsible. It was then inadvisable for me, or any of my household, to appear on the streets, whether for fetching up water from the river, or for any other purpose.[8]

---

8 [FW] The second half of the nineteenth century was traumatic: as the Manchu Qing Dynasty declined and foreign pressure increased, there were disastrous

66

But in the early days the river was our only source of supply. It was one of the coolie's routine duties to go down daily to the river-side, fill his wooden buckets, and bring his heavy load home suspended from his carrying pole. The journey would have to be repeated several times. Arrived home the water was poured into large earthenware receptacles, or K'angs, and allowed to settle. The addition of alum facilitated the deposit of mud and other suspended matter, and clarified it. But this process did not rid the water of the germs of disease with which it was teeming. Typhoid, dysentery, and cholera were endemic, and would at times break out in raging epidemics. There was a large boat population, whose insanitary habits left very much to be desired. Thus the river was constantly being polluted by the floating community. Knowing nothing of the microbic origin of disease water was drunk without any attempt at purification. Thus it was that in the heat of the summer, when the high temperature favoured the multiplication of water-borne disease germs, epidemics would break out of a virulence and of a magnitude not known in Western countries. And this in spite of the fact that, by the repeated ingestion of these germs, a high degree of immunity had been acquired by the people since childhood.

Fortunately the incidence of disease is lessened also by the Chinese habit of drinking tea. This requires previous boiling of the water, and the consequent destruction of the causative micro-organism. So tea has been a God-send to China. It has been, through the centuries, and still is, the means of preserving countless lives; though this fact is not realised by the people. Nevertheless, despite such protection as is afforded by acquired immunity and by the tea-drinking habit, the mortality from these intestinal affections is appalling. Tens of thousands may perish in the city in a single epidemic.

---

rebellions, such as that of the Taipings, who devastated southern and central China between 1850 and 1864, and the Nian rebellion (1851–68) in northern China. The latter was largely a response to devastating floods caused by the Yellow River bursting its banks. Coinciding with the arrivals of strangers, it is possible that they were sometimes considered responsible. Certainly, opposition to railway construction (by foreigners) involved a fear of the unknown and a fear that they would interfere with the local geomancy, or *fengshui*, which, it was believed, would bring disaster.

To foreigners, whose resistance against infections is lower, the danger is very much greater; though, with regard to typhoid, inoculation affords a high degree of protection. I never drank cold un-boiled water in China, unless it was from a mountain spring. The strictest rule in the house is that, after standing and clearing, every drop of water must be boiled. In this matter, in spite of all our vigilance, we are very much in the hands of our servants, and many indeed have been the tragedies resulting from the employment of an unreliable staff.

There is a very irritating Chinese phrase – 'T'sa-puh-to' [chabuduo] – a phrase which is in constant use. Literally it means 'Not much difference', or, as we would say, 'near enough'.[9] If you order the making of a garment, or a piece of furniture, or the performance of some task, the work may be done well up to a point, but at the end there is a 'lack of finish'. When you point out the imperfection, or express disappointment at the incompleteness of the job, there is surprise that you should complain of so small a matter. Surely it is 'near enough'. If it is 'ts'a-puh-to', that should satisfy, whether it be in building a house or in boiling an egg. In those early days I was constantly up against this attitude of satisfaction with inferior standards, and I realised its potential dangers. I was determined that with regard to the sterilisation of my water, at any rate, there was to be no 'ts'a-puh-to'. No mere heating would suffice. It was to be *boiled* for five minutes by the clock. Early contests and victories over the purification of the water led to further triumphs in other fields, until, in the process of time, 'ts'a-puh-to', though always a factor to be reckoned with, ceased to be such a productive source of irritation and expostulation.

---

9 [FW] *chabuduo* means 'almost' or, as Peake says, 'near enough'.

68

# Chapter VI

# A Call on the Tao-t'ai

I had barely got comfortably settled down in my new abode when one morning Ah-shin came excitedly into my room bearing a large red visiting card and announced, with an air which betokened the importance of the occasion, that the chief magistrate of the city, His Excellency the Tao-t'ai had arrived for the purpose of paying a formal call. The Ta-ren ('Great Man') seated in his handsome sedan-chair and accompanied by his liveried retinue, was even then at the front gate.[10] I gave orders for the gates to be thrown open, and for his Excellency to be escorted up to my guest-room. Very soon he arrived, resplendent in his mandarin robes and hat, attended by several of his immediate suite.

After the usual polite greetings I bowed my distinguished visitor into the chief seat, and tried to express my appreciation of his courtesy in calling on me. He was very affable, and asked many questions relating to foreign countries and customs. It was evident that he was puzzled as to my reasons for leaving my own 'honourable' mother-land and coming to live thus alone in his 'contemptible' country. My vocabulary was very limited, but in a few words I explained that I was a doctor, and that as such I hoped to be of service to his people. To all appearances he heartily approved. At this point Ah-shin appeared, in clean blue gown and neatly plaited pigtail, with the inevitable tea. After this final move the great man rose to go, and, in spite of his remonstrances, I escorted him to the gate, where, watched by a big crowd which had collected in the street during our interview, we took formal leave of each other.

---

10  [FW] The Tao-t'ai (Daotai) was the local magistrate, referred to as the Ta-ren (Daren) or 'Great Man'.

I was glad the Tao-t'ai had been, and that his bearing though punctilious had been friendly. As the Chief Mandarin of the city on him devolved the responsibility of maintaining law and order. The gesture would not be lost on the populace.

It now became my duty to return his call, although, with my restricted knowledge of the language and of Chinese etiquette, it was an ordeal from which I would gladly have been excused.

His Excellency was duly informed of my intention, and on the morning appointed for my visit just as I was about to set forth, I was surprised by the arrival of a guard of soldiers. They had been despatched by His Excellency to escort me to his official residence, or 'Yamen'. The crowd fell back as they noted that the foreign devil was under the protection of the Chief Magistrate's own body-guard. There were no insulting remarks, or any kind of hostile demonstration. The crowd was quick to understand the Tao-t'ai's plain hint that order would be enforced.

On arrival at the Yamen my chair was borne through huge wooden gates, guarded by sentries, and past the most fearsome-looking lions carved in stone. Just beyond the lions, and right in our path, was a blank wall, the purpose of which was to obstruct the passage of evil spirits, which are thought to travel only in straight lines. Making a detour around the 'devil-screen' we passed on through lines of attendants until an inner courtyard was reached. Here my visiting card (an oblong of scarlet paper measuring 8" by 4", and bearing the three characters in black which composed my Chinese name) was handed to an orderly and borne aloft with great ceremony to the 'great man' in the inner reception hall. Soon the word came to advance. My chair was lowered. I stepped out, and was courteously escorted into the guest chamber.

The Tao-t'ai was standing to receive me. He was fully attired in his official robes as a Mandarin of high rank. I particularly admired the square of silken embroidery covering the front of the outer garment. Bringing both hands together, lifting them up to the forehead and then lowering them, we bowed low to each other. After this he led me forward and politely indicated that he wished me to take a seat in the place of honour on the raised dais. My role now was to back away, and to show great reluctance, as being unworthy of such high regard. Then followed the customary by-play, he pressing me forward I hanging back. When I judged there had been sufficient ceremonial dumb-show to satisfy the requirements of good manners, I modestly took one of the two high seats. His Excellency thereupon immediately occupied the other. Between us was a low table on which was spread the pipe and paraphernalia for smoking opium. With a gesture my host indicated to an attendant that he wished these removed, and ordered tea to be brought.

The tea was served very hot, and without milk or sugar, in beautiful porcelain cups. Each cup, of a small tea-bowl shape, was without handle. It was furnished with a lid, and rested on a metal saucer. On the surface of the tea there floated a small dried flower, which, under the influence of the heat and the steam, slowly unfolded its petals and emitted a delightful fragrance. A little tea had spilled over into my saucer. His Excellency noticing this, rose, took up the cup and having whisked the offending liquid on the floor, returned it to me with both hands and a bow. This I took to be a token of marked courtesy, and it was evidently so regarded by all present.

In view of the language difficulty conversation was not easy. This was made still more embarrassing for me by the presence of a numerous audience – officials of lower rank, soldiers, yamen-runners, and retainers – who stood and lined the walls down both sides of the guest-hall. When a courier arrived from without having a report to make, he would come before the Tao-t'ai, drop down on one knee, and so deliver his dispatch or his tidings. All were silent, intently listening to every word spoken, and obviously keenly interested. There was studied decorum; not even an amused smile, though I was conscious that I cut but a sorry figure, and that my efforts to converse must have been distinctly amusing.

It was a strange scene. We sat enthroned on the dais, while His Excellency's entourage, so strikingly oriental in dress and feature, made an impressive and colourful array. On the walls were lively pictures, for the most part realistic portrayals of irate mandarins brandishing mighty swords, and of unbelievable ferocity. But there were also some beautiful examples of Chinese art; mainly rural scenes – workers in the rice fields, a boatman fishing, wild duck on the wing, and so on; all exquisitely drawn in ink with the finely painted native brush.

At last, to my infinite relief, the Tao-t'ai raised his cup to his lips. I immediately did the same, for this signalled that the call was at an end.

At this point, except for two or three in personal attendance on His Excellency, there was a general dispersal, officials, soldiers, and henchmen all smartly moved off on their several duties. The word was passed along that the interview was over. Outside there was a loud shout of 'chiou-fu' – calling the chair-bearers to stand by. Replacing our cups the Tao-t'ai and I rose. In spite of my polite remonstrance 'Ta-ren puh sung' meaning 'Your Excellency must not trouble to escort me', he insisted on accompanying me along the covered way and under the swinging lanterns, to the outer precinct. There in the courtyard my sedan-chair was already manned and waiting. We made our mutual obeisance, and I took my seat. Instantly I was hoisted to the height of the men's shoulders. There was a shout of 'Kai-mou' ['Kaimen'] – 'Open the gates' – and I was borne out into the street between two lines of Yamen-guards, some of whom were detached to escort me home. Outside the gates an eager and expectant throng had gathered. It was evident that the word had been passed round in the neighbourhood that the Western barbarian was paying a call on the Tao-t'ai. Swinging out into the road-way, my advance guard armed with truncheons, and shouting 'Kai-lo' – 'Clear the way!' – caused the crowd to fall back, and so opened up a lane for the chair-bearers. We passed down the thoroughfare at a rapid rate. There were some black looks and muttered curses, but beyond a clod or two heaved from behind, there was not, on this occasion, any more-marked manifestations of ill-will. I reached home without further incident.

It was not very long after my call related above, that the Tao-t'ai, wishing, as a Confucian scholar, to observe the injunctions of the great sage regarding the correct attitude to be adopted towards aliens, and anxious to set an example before his people of hospitality to the stranger, invited me to a feast at his official residence.

As before, His Excellency despatched a squad of soldiers to ensure my safe conduct through the streets. Arrived at the Yamen I was treated with the same ceremony as on the former occasion, but once in his private room all formality was dropped. Here I was introduced to several of his friends whom he had also invited.

Very soon an attendant came and announced that the table was spread. We passed into an adjoining room, in the centre of which was a round table covered with numerous dishes of steaming viands. Taking our place our distinguished host pressed us to help ourselves. The other guests were not slow to respond, reaching out to sample one dish after another, and wielding their chop-sticks with great dexterity. I made a valiant effort to follow suit, but found the chop-sticks most difficult to manipulate. It is not easy for the unpractised hand to extract, with the aid of two slender ivory rods, a slippery pigeon's egg floating in a bowl of gravy. Noticing my awkwardness my neighbours came to my rescue, selecting particular tit-bits and transferring them to my porcelain spoon. It would never have occurred to them that it might be distasteful to me that they should for this purpose use implements which had already been in their own mouths!

The fare was very rich and good, and the cooking excellent. The menu included duck, chicken, fish, shark's fin, sea-slugs, porpoise, pigeons' eggs, bird's nest soup, bamboo-shoots, lotus-lily seeds, and rice.

The birds' nest soup was quite a speciality, and was certainly very tasty. I believe it is quite a laborious task to prepare it. The nests are built of sea-weed by a species of swallow and come from the coastal areas of China.[11] They are of a gelatinous consistence and on this account are much contaminated by the birds' feathers, every one of which must be carefully removed before the nests are boiled to prepare the soup.

The feast was protracted to an interminable length; but when at last it came to its conclusion we returned to the same private room, and the conversation à propos the state of the crops, foreign countries, travel etc. continued.

---

11 [FW] Birds' nest soup is actually made from swallows' nests, made from swallows' saliva or spit!

Tea was brought. His Excellency, a very stout man, smoked his long pipe, drawing the tobacco smoke with a bubbling sound through water in a metal container. He appeared somnolent (after his heavy meal), contented, and at peace with all the world.

I made several moves to go, but was persuaded not to hurry. At length, after thanking His Excellency for his kind hospitality, I was permitted to take my leave, and was accompanied by him to the outer court, where my chair and the military escort were in readiness. As I passed through the main gateway I turned and saw my host still standing, and courteously awaiting my final disappearance.

There were other occasions on which I met with civility and good-will; but such, in those early days, were the exception and not the rule. The general bearing of the populace was one of hostility, and I had perforce to live a very secluded life. In spite of this I had many opportunities of observing the people, their characteristics, their mental outlook, and their manner of life.

I was particularly interested in everything pertaining to Chinese medical practice. It soon became abundantly clear that it was riddled through and through with superstition, and that it rested on no scientific basis. There was in consequence an appalling amount of avoidable suffering. It seemed to me there could be no more necessitous field to which to bring some of the blessings of modern medicine and surgery; and yet, owing to the prejudiced attitude of the people, the prospect of opening up medical work among them seemed very far distant. As to the fulfilment of my ambition to build a hospital for this city of one quarter of a million inhabitants, the outlook appeared remote indeed.

# Chapter VII

# THE CHINESE DOCTOR

We have now in China a few medical schools under foreign tutelage which are doing excellent work in training students on Western lines. But these are of comparatively recent origin. It will be many years before they can supply the vast population with even a fraction of the number of qualified doctors which are needed. So among the uncounted millions of the interior it is still the same as it has ever been. Anyone is free to don a long robe, purchase a pair of large horn-rimmed spectacles, lay in a stock of dried herbs and bones, and proclaim himself a doctor!

There were, however, differences in grade and reputation among the practitioners. The better sort, and those who pretended to be guided by some sort of 'system', relied on the theory of 'the five elements' – gold, wood, water, fire, and earth. According to this hypothesis these elements are all represented in the human body. If they are in combination in the right proportions then the balance is correct, and the body is in health. Sickness is due to the balance having been upset by one or more of the elements preponderating over the others, and the proper equilibrium therefore deranged. The object of the physician is to discover which of the five components has got out of control, and to bring it back to its right proportion by administering the correct antidote. If the patient is hot and feverish it is obvious that the fire constituent over-rides the others, and water must be applied within and without to reduce it to its correct relative position, and so restore the balance.

But it is not always so evident as to which element *has* got out of hand, and then the physician arrives at his diagnosis, in some mysterious manner, by feeling the pulses. Both pulses must be felt simultaneously.[12] No questions are asked. The prescription is then written.

Frequently the prescriptions are family heirlooms, and handed down from father to son; they must be kept a dead secret. Particularly is this the case when doctoring has been the family calling for generations. Such families have a special reputation, and the more remote the medical tradition the more highly honoured is the physician.

But these more respectable ones, who attempt to be guided by some sort of conventional system, are relatively few. Their ideas to our minds, may be ignorant and foolish, but they are at least striving to follow the teachings of an ancient philosophy to the best of their ability.

It was not so with the vast majority of the medical fraternity. Native practice, which when analysed resolves itself into a blend of knavery, devil-exorcism, and superstition, was in the hands of charlatans and quacks. With them disease is attributed to the anger of the gods, or to possession by evil spirits. The former may perhaps be appeased by sacrificial oblations; and the latter expelled by the use of charms, or scared away by gongs and fire-crackers. If the 'doctor' has pronounced the malady as being due to an evil spirit he may prescribe such drastic treatment as beating or needling the patient to expel the demon. Or he may write a few magic characters on a slip of scarlet paper. This the patient must burn, make a decoction of the ashes, and swallow the draught. The mystic writing, acting as a charm, will cast a spell upon the intruder and dislodge him.

It would be impossible to recount the many strange ideas and superstitions which are held to be potent in the cure of the sick. It is commonly believed that if a piece of the flesh of a devoted member of the family be excised, cooked, and administered to the patient, it will be sure to result in his or her recovery. I personally knew a woman, who, when a girl, cut off a slice of the fleshy part of her forearm in her desperate anxiety to save her dying mother.

But the 'quack' will also have his stall on the street, for a large proportion

---

12 [ECP] The Chinese often ask why we feel only one pulse; and why we ask so many questions. This surely is proof of our incompetence. The pulses ought to have told us everything.

of his income is derived from the sale of his medicaments and plasters. His stock-in-trade consists of dried herbs, seeds, fungi, shells, pebbles, chalk, mica, and the like, from the vegetable and mineral kingdom. Drugs of animal origin are less pure, and sometimes disgusting. They include those obtained from all sorts of reptiles, snakes, scorpions, centipedes, insects, and also animal excreta. Bones, too, are in common use. The crushed bones of a tiger are highly valued for general debility; the idea being that the bones of such a powerful creature, when prescribed for a weakly patient, must necessarily increase his physical strength. Tiger bone, and rhinoceros horn, are expensive of course. These dangerous animals being unwilling to part with portions of their anatomy for the good of mankind, the supply is limited and the price high.

It is a good line also to lay in a stock of small living things, such as ear-wigs and beetles. These come in very handy, on occasion. When tinkering around an aching tooth, deftly to produce (from up a capacious sleeve) a live grub, and to demonstrate this as the cause of the trouble, adds greatly to the kudos of the practitioners.

Ignorance and superstition enter just as largely in native 'surgical' practice (if one may be allowed to use the term) as in medical. Here again the malady is ascribed to demoniacal possession, and the point to be considered is the line of treatment best calculated to result in the eviction of the malign spirit. Needles are a favourite choice, and are very frequently resorted to, for this purpose. They are used either cold or heated, and may be thrust into any part of the body, including the abdominal cavity and the eye-ball. Countless eyes have been ruined by needle puncture. I have known of a dirty skewer being driven into a child's tubercular knee, with the object of prodding out the demon; resulting of course in septic poisoning and total destruction of the joint. By the time such a case reaches the foreign doctor amputation of the limb may offer the only chance of saving the patient's life.

It was very evident that the lot of those unfortunate enough to fall sick was pitiable in the extreme: to add to their need of proper care was the further misery occasioned by the crude methods employed by their own doctors. The patience and fortitude with which such suffering was borne was equally evident.

From these remarks, and I have touched but lightly on the subject, it will be appreciated how abysmal is the ignorance, how thick the darkness, in which the people grope. Notwithstanding her ancient civilisation, in all branches of scientific knowledge China is still many centuries behind the times. It is doubtful if the pursuit of medicine, as conducted by the generability of native practitioners, can claim any advance on the black magic and diablerie of the African witch-doctor.

In common with other Chinese cities there was nothing, of course, in Heng-chow, in the nature of a public health service. No pure water supply, no hospitals, no organised sanitary system, no isolation of infectious disease. It was no uncommon sight to see cases of small-pox and leprosy in the streets. I have mentioned the indescribably offensive street-gutters into which all kinds of filth and garbage could be thrown. Sewage was collected from these gutters, and from open pits, and carried away by coolies in large wooden tubs to be used as manure for their vegetable gardens. There was no obligation on anybody to do this, and no payment was made for it. It was a mutual convenience. Collectors were glad to get the fertiliser, and the townspeople were glad to have it partially removed. If it were not for this co-operation between town and country the insanitary state of the city, bad as it was, would have been unspeakable.[13]

Terrible epidemics of the water-borne diseases, especially of cholera, broke out from time to time. With these the civil authorities and the native physicians, having no idea of the cause, were helpless to cope.

The popular view was that these dreaded visitations were due to the 'luck' of the city having been 'stolen' – perhaps by the foreigner – or were the work of malevolent spirits who must be appeased. In consequence (as also in drought, famine, or flood) processions were organised, and the idols were carried shoulder-high through the streets. These parades through the city were very tawdry affairs. Men and boys, gaudily attired, would head the procession beating gongs and tin-cans.

13 [ECP] I speak of China as I found her. It is true that, of late years, from the lands of the 'outer barbarians', beams of light have penetrated into some of the great centres of population. But an ancient and conservative country does not respond readily to foreign ideas and innovations; there can be no doubt that, over the vast extent of the Empire, the same ignorance and superstition prevails, and the same deplorable practices obtain, in the treatment of the sick.

Then would come the idol, seated high in his canopied chair, and after him more gongs and drums. These would be followed by the priests, in showy robes, chanting their prayers and invocations. Sometimes, when day followed day and pestilence continued unabated, the rage of the people would rise against the idols. There were times when these wooden images would be attacked and beaten in the street. In times of drought the canopy over the rain-god might be torn down so that he could feel the blistering heat of the sun. 'Now perhaps you know what it feels like!' the people shout. 'How do you like frizzling in the sun with never a drop of rain?' 'Can't you see how the crops perish?' Thus anxious entreaty would at length break down and give place to violence, petulance, and abuse.[14]

With regard to floods much of the trouble could have been avoided by proper embankment of the river irrigation, and forestry. If, as might happen on very rare occasions, a grant was made for public work of this kind from Peking, a high percentage of the money would stick to the hands of the officials through whom it passed; each would take his quota, until by the time it reached the local contractors commissioned to undertake the job, only a bit of patch-work could be done. It would be the same if funds were raised by a tax levied on the people. This was accepted as in the natural and traditional order of things. It had always been so. The toiling millions had always been the sufferers. As their own proverb put it, 'The big fish eat the little fish, the little fish eat still smaller fish, the smallest fish eat mud!'

Thus there was but little help to be expected from above. With regard to the population as a whole, no preventive measures were taken to safe-guard them from disaster; and as to the individual, he was indeed in a sorry plight, when, overtaken by bodily disability or disease, he had no one but the specious and ignorant charlatan to whom he could turn.

---

14 [ECP] In one place (into which a smattering of foreign ideas had infiltrated), as the pièce de résistance, a paraffin tin, filled with a weak solution of Jeyes' fluid, was carried suspended from a pole between a couple of coolies. The rear one periodically dipped a bunch of twigs into the tin and clicked a sprinkling of the fluid towards the houses on either side. This was the foreign 'disease-destroying charm'. It was as well to have two strings to one's bow. If appeals to the idol were fruitless, perhaps the foreign medicine might do the trick!

# Chapter VIII

# PREPARATORY STUDIES

My home Society had made me grants, both for the purchase of the premises which I now occupied, and for necessary equipment of drugs, dressings, and surgical instruments which I required. These goods were now on the way to me.

At Hankow they would be transferred from the river-steamer to a native junk and could travel to me all the way by water.

Pending their arrival there were certain alterations to be made in the pavilions of the forward court in order to make them completely suitable for the purposes of an out-patient practice. Furniture for these rooms, including shelving for the dispensary, and a few simple wooden beds for the 'ward', had to be provided. All this could be done locally. In due course all was ready, and then at last the big consignment reached me.

There followed many busy days – unpacking, sorting, arranging. Ah-shin was a real help. While working he would ask many questions concerning the uses of the strange things he was handling. He was quite sure, that, with the opening of the out-patient premises, we would be besieged by crowds of importunate patients, and this to him was an exhilarating prospect. Chow-ling was by no means so sanguine. He regarded the enterprise as fraught with the most sinister, not to say tragic, possibilities. In his view it was much more likely that we would have the whole place stormed and looted by a furious mob, and that we would be lucky if we escaped with our lives. I must confess that

I found Chow-ling's opinion rather disturbing; for though naturally of a lugubrious temperament, his judgment was the riper and the more reliable.

But much yet remained to be done before I could think of opening my doors. It would be wiser not to be in a hurry. I would live quietly at home, occasionally appear on the street, and pass the time of day in friendly manner whenever opportunity offered.

Perhaps in time the people would get used to my presence, and their animosity towards the foreigner diminish.

While waiting it was imperative to push forward with my study of the language, which was difficult and required close application. I had early engaged a local scholar as tutor. Every morning he came to my room and we toiled on together. The language is monosyllabic, and many of the monosyllabic sounds are difficult to pronounce. Each sound represents a word, which is expressed in writing by its own special ideogram – a combination of straight and curved strokes. These strokes, made with the Chinese writing-brush held vertically, may be few or many. It is quite common to have as many as a dozen, or more, strokes to a character. This may give some idea of the magnitude of the task of learning to read and write these strange hieroglyphics, which number many thousands.

A few are readily learnt. For example, it is easy to remember that two legs represent 'man' (ren), written thus. In remote times no doubt a more complete picture of a man was in vogue, but for many centuries only his legs have remained. The ideogram for 'prisoner' is a man in a cage, written thus. A 'roof' (mien) is written so (suggestive of roof and chimney); a 'pig' (shi) so (not at all suggestive). Put a pig under a roof and we have the character for 'home', written thus.

A 'woman' (nu) is written so. A woman under a roof gives us the character (nigan), which means 'peace and quiet'. Two women under one roof, represent 'strife, discord'. Three women under one roof – 'gossip, scandal'. What could be better than for a mother to have a son? And so the character for 'good' (hao) is made up of woman and son, and is written so. The ideogram also means 'to love, to be fond of'. (keo) = 'a mouth', (er) = 'an ear', (men) = 'a gate, a door', (wen) = 'to ask, to beg' – i.e. a mouth at the gate. (wen) = 'to hear, to listen'; i.e. an ear at the door (both 'wen' but spoken in different tones).[15]

Such ideograms are easy to learn, but the vast majority are difficult and require a great effort of memory. The character with its sound and its meaning, must all be memorised. It is even more difficult to so recall its visual image as to be able to write it. The monosyllabic sounds are, to our ears, uncouth, and it is not easy to spell them so as to give a correct idea of their pronunciation. Counting from 1 to 10 sounds are as follows: ee, er, san, sz, oo, lo, chee, ba, jo, shi. The first sentence of the Lord's Prayer would be : Nge, mun, dzai, t'ien, shang, tih, fu. But the chief difficulty in learning these sounds (along with their corresponding characters and meaning) is in remembering the correct inflexion of voice with which they must be spoken. There are five principal voice-modulations, or 'tones'. It is essential, in using a word, that it be spoken in the correct tone. If a wrong tone is used it will have a different meaning. The sound 'yen' may mean a 'word', or it may mean 'salt', or 'strict' or an 'eye', or scores of other meanings, each with its own tone, and with its differently written character. There are less than three hundred sounds in the language, each with its many meanings; but as there are only five principal tones it is obvious that many of them must have the same tone. Then how is one to understand what is being said, and how is this shortage of words made up? It is made up, not only by the use of the correct tone, but also by coupling together two words of different sound but of similar meaning. For

---

15 The characters for man 人,prisoner 囚, pig 猪,and home 家 are accurately described. The radical (part of a character) which stands for 'roof' is not used on its own and I have not been able to identify the term 'mian' for 'roof' which may be a local usage. 女 is the character for woman, and peace is indeed composed as Dr. Peake suggests (a 'roof' over a woman) 安, as is the character for 'good' or 'to love, be fond of' 好 (mother and son). Mouth 口 and ear 耳 and gate 门 are used as he describes, to form the characters for 'to ask' 问 or 'to hear' 闻. There is no word composed of two 'woman' characters although it is true that three 'women' combined (though now written thus: 奸) means 'wicked' or 'treacherous' or 'illicit sexual relations'. Though such simple pictographic characters amuse foreign learners of Chinese, they represent a tiny portion of the 44,000 characters in the seventeenth-century Kangxi dictionary and the subtlety and complexity of the language is not best exemplified by such examples.

instance, if we take the word 'yen' again, meaning an 'eye', by adding another word 't'sing'(bright, clear) we get the combination yen-ts'ing, which could only mean an 'eye'. Or, very often, one must understand simply from the context.

I started work with my teacher, and a ponderous dictionary, on the less difficult Chinese books, beginning with that known as Tri-metrical Classics. This has a 3-character metre, arranged in couplets, and goes with a swing. The first couplet proclaims that 'Man, at his beginning, / Was, by nature, originally good' – a rather striking assertion to find in an ancient pagan classic.

Later I went on to study 'The Sacred Edict'; 'The Book of Rewards and Punishments'; 'The Great Learning'; 'The Works of Mencius' and 'The Confucian Analects'. There is much that is arresting in the sayings of China's great sage, Confucius; but it is sadly obscured in a mass of trivial verbiage. The sayings of the master that have been preserved resolve themselves into rules for correct conduct. Gems there are; such as 'What you do not like when done to yourself, do not do to others'; and 'What the superior man seeks is in himself, what the small man seeks is in others' – but they must be searched for and extracted from much that is trifling and worthless.

I realised quite early that I not only had to learn, but I should also have to teach. When my medical work started I would require assistants. Besides the gate-keeper, whose duty it would be to marshal the patients in their proper order in the waiting-room, I would require at least two others, one to assist me in the consulting-room and one to act as dispenser. This meant preliminary training, but the difficulty was to find suitable candidates. It required some courage to associate oneself with the foreigner. Ultimately I succeeded in engaging two youths whom I judged to be full of promise. Subsequent history was to prove that I was wrong with regard to one of these, but the other more than fulfilled my expectations. His name was Lei.

So in addition to my Chinese studies, I set to work to instruct these two students in the elements of anatomy, physiology, and pharmacy. It was hard work; for I had myself to discover the Chinese names for the different parts and organs of the body, and try to explain their functions.

The boys collected specimens of frogs, which we dissected together. The circulation of the blood was a revelation. We spread the web of a live frog's foot on the stage of my microscope, and to actually see the blood corpuscles coursing through the capillaries amazed them.

Teaching them the foreign drugs and how to dispense them, was perhaps the most difficult. Here there was no Chinese equivalent for the names which occur in our Western materia medica (except in a very few instances, such as opium), so it was necessary for them to learn to read and write the Latin names. This required mastery of our alphabet to begin with. Then came prescription reading. They soon learnt how to interpret the signs, to weigh solids, and to measure liquids correctly.

As time went on other assistants had to be trained. One of the original two turned out to be of poor quality, and eventually it was necessary to discharge him; but young Lei showed remarkable aptitude from the first. He had intelligence far above the average and rapidly absorbed all instruction. His father was a scholar and a man of upright character, and the son had inherited his father's high principles of conduct. With all his natural ability Lei was of a most modest disposition; an attractive and lovable personality. Perhaps I might here anticipate events in stating that he was to become my right-hand man for over twenty years. Those early beginnings were destined to lead to a distinguished and most useful career. There were five years when I had to do without his help. That was when he was taking a full course of study at our Medical School in Hankow; where, among other selected students, he proved himself *facile princeps*. As the years went by Lei developed into a thoughtful and able physician, a skillful surgeon, and an ardent laboratory worker and microscopist. He was one of the ten talent people, to whom nothing appeared difficult. When I married, my wife taught him English. In time he was able to write a very good letter and could correspond with us when away. She also taught him music, and to play the organ. Watercolour painting was another of his accomplishments. This was of great service to him in his anatomical drawings, which were beautifully executed. An American professor, seeing some of his coloured plates in Hankow, expressed the opinion that they would adorn any modern text-book on anatomy.

The secret of Lei's influence lay not only in his intellectual gifts – enhanced as these were by his quiet and unassuming personality. The foundation of his sterling character was his conviction of the truth of Christianity. He embraced this religion for himself; and in his own attractive, unobtrusive way he brought many others to the same Faith. Living in a heathen environment one came against much that was debased and sordid, but in Dr Lei China could show a man of the finest type, an honour to any country. There is no need to despair of a land which is capable of producing such men.

# Chapter IX

# SOME TRAITS IN THE CHINESE CHARACTER

Perhaps I might be allowed to interrupt my narrative at this point to introduce some remarks on what appeared to me to be salient features in the life and character of the people among whom I had made my home.

The Chinese are, at first, difficult to understand. Between them and the foreigner there is, seemingly, 'A great gulf fixed'. But the chasm is more apparent than real. It is, in large measure, due to the language difficulty. Then once the language is mastered a bridge has been thrown across the gulf, communications opened, and we can get at each other in a way previously found to be impossible. We then find that they are essentially a very human people. They have the same needs, feelings, and emotions as the rest of mankind. Nevertheless they have their own distinctive characteristics. These characteristics comprise so complex an assortment, and are often so apparently contradictory, that any remarks which I may make are necessarily of a most incomplete and fragmentary nature; yet they are, I think, the things which are most likely to strike any foreigner who settles down among them and has the opportunity of close observation.

The first thing to force itself so unpleasantly upon my attention – I speak of 50 years ago – was the universal contempt, in which the foreigner was held by all sections of the people. Although China ranked among the backward nations of the earth, she was at the same time the most conceited. The attitude of her Government to the Foreign

Powers was one of arrogant condescension.[16] We were regarded as 'outer barbarians', and 'foreign devils'. It was not until 1860, after much protest and expostulation, that the term 'barbarian 'was excluded from diplomatic documents. We appeared uncultured in their eyes. We could not speak their language, we could not read their books. We were unacquainted with the teachings of their ancient philosophers. We were ignorant of social etiquette. We did not observe correct 'form', or say the right things at the right time; and the way we handled the chop-sticks, though regarded with polite gravity by our hosts, must have been a sheer joy to the attendants, who no doubt reproduced our unskilful efforts to the delight of their comrades in the back-quarters.

But did not the foreigners' superior achievements in science impress them?

Not at all. They knew very little of the wonders of steam and electricity; and the tales they had heard, if true, would only be attributed to the foreign devils' uncanny magic. What was good enough for their revered ancestors was good enough for them.

On all scientific matters, even the most elementary, I found profound ignorance. One night when an eclipse of the moon was due, I was alarmed by the most awful din. The people, with one accord, had turned out of their houses into the streets and were beating gongs, brass-ware, and any pots and pans they could seize, in order to create pandemonium. What did it mean? Was it the pre-arranged signal for an attack on the foreigner? No. Chow-ling soon set my mind at rest on that score. 'The dog of the skies', he said, was gnawing at the moon,

---

16 [FW] Peake's view of the Chinese government's attitude as one of 'arrogant condescension' could equally well be applied to that of the British government towards China and its territorial rights and the utter superiority of Western ways. His remarks on Chinese music and architecture are resolutely Eurocentric, whilst he reproves the Chinese for Sinocentricity. Though it is true that the citizens of inland, isolated Hengyang [Heng-chow] had no knowledge of science as he understood it, he seems unaware of the receptiveness of the Chinese of the eastern seaboard to Western science. He is right to state here and in subsequent passages that China had achieved much in previous millennia, and various experts such as Joseph Needham and Mark Elvin have attempted to explain China's failure to 'progress' (in Western terms). The problem, for China, was the aggressive intrusion of the Western nations, armed with the latest weapons and determined to enforce trade (in tea, porcelain and silks) on Western terms, as well as force the country open to Christian missionaries.

and would swallow it, so every one must turn out and help in the uproar to frighten the dog and make him disgorge. The plan had always proved successful!

On a later occasion the time drew near for a reappearance of Halley's Comet, which made its terrestrial visitation once every 75 years. An eclipse of the moon was a well-known phenomenon; but a brilliant awe-inspiring spectacle, such as Halley's Comet was reputed to be, was calculated to arouse the greatest excitement. Consternation and fear would seize the populace. The apparition would be taken as a portent of ominous significance; perhaps of war, or famine, or some other great national calamity. A scape-goat would be sought. Who was responsible? Was it the foreigners? It was they who by their diabolical arts were bringing ruination upon the country. 'Rout them out! Burn down their houses! Kill them!' That was the danger that loomed ahead.

Fortunately, some far-seeing missionaries 1,000 miles away in Shanghai, realising the peril to their nationals in inland places, had had posters printed in Chinese explaining the periodical return of the comet as a natural phenomenon, and stating the time when it was next due. An illustration gave a rough idea of its appearance. I sent to Shanghai for a number of copies and had them posted up in the streets. The comet came at its appointed time some weeks later; but the danger had been forestalled, and there was no trouble. I was free to enjoy the magnificent spectacle in peace. Its glowing 'head', and the broad phosphorescent tail streaming right across the heavens was of unexpected brilliance and has left a lasting impression on my mind.

It is difficult to understand such profound ignorance in the most elementary facts of science in such an ancient and intelligent people. It is sometimes asserted that China was highly civilised many hundreds of years before occidental peoples had emerged from a state of barbarism. Undoubtedly, through the ages, China had evolved her own pattern of civilisation. The Chinese originated the silk industry over 2,000 years B.C., many centuries before it reached Europe. They invented their own ideograms to represent words, thus reducing their spoken language to writing, they discovered how to make paper – although to this day, of a very inferior quality – and how to print on it by means of wooden type. Their arts and crafts touch a high level of achievement, particularly in sculpture; in finely wrought work in gold, silver, jade, and ivory; in pottery and porcelain, in very lovely silk embroidery. Some of China's artists are famous for their exquisite draughtsmanship. But when we come to music, she struck me as surprisingly backward, her music, if music it can be called, being of a singularly crude and primitive type. With regard to architecture, there is some beautiful work – but on a small scale, and very much on the same modes. There is nothing to compare with the finest Western architecture, as exemplified, for instance, in our great cathedrals.

It has been said that a country's civilisation may be gauged by its means of transport, and by its roads. If this be true we would be compelled to give China a very low place in the scale. I found no 'roads', such as we understand the term, but only tracks so narrow that it was usually necessary to travel on them in single file.[17]

From the records and relics of the past one comes to the conclusion that China's highest productiveness belongs to the bygone age. At a certain period, difficult to determine, stagnation, and rot set in. In the sciences she does not appear to have progressed at all. Regarding medicine all one can say is that there are a few herbs which have real value. These were evidently stumbled upon from empirical trial, and not revealed by scientific investigation of the medicinal prop-erties latent within the vegetable kingdom. One of them, said to have been used in China as long as 4,000 years ago, is the grass-like plant ma-huang. It is from ma-huang that our chemists have extracted the active principle ephedrine, used in the treatment of asthma and other respiratory disorders.

How is it that China's 4,000 years of civilisation have not resulted in a higher culture, and that she has not had more to contribute to the modern world?

I think the answer to this is to be found, to a large extent, in the fact that for untold centuries she has been held fast in the paralysing grip

---

17 [ECP] This was certainly the case in central and southern China. On the dusty plains of the north I afterwards became acquainted with the Peking mule-cart, which requires a somewhat wider track; in the dry season all dust, and in the wet deep mud.

of senseless superstition. Her religions have done nothing to free her from this tyrannical stronghold. Life is riddled through and through with these frightening and enslaving delusions. Feng-shui, the 'spirits of wind and water', must always be reckoned with. Before any family event the soothsayer must be consulted to advise on the lucky day. Even the dead must remain unburied in their coffins, it may be for months, until the auspicious day arrives. Useful works for the public good must be disallowed – they might disturb the feng-shui and bring calamity. When, under foreign supervision, an effort was first made to lay a much needed railway, the lines were torn up by an infuriated mob, who believed that the spirits would be incensed and that trouble would ensue for the people. China has great mineral wealth, but mining could not be undertaken because to dig deep holes into the earth would release terrifying dragons whose fiery breath would spread pestilence far and wide. With superstitions such as these how could there be growth in knowledge or any scientific progress?

With regards to manners the Chinese certainly cannot be classed as uncivilised. Among their many good qualities is courtesy, or, as they themselves would express it, propriety. I found that, taken by himself (if he were your patient or your guest, or if you were *his* guest) the Chinese, be he gentleman or coolie, was always polite and respectful. It was when one encountered the crowd that things were more apt to take an ugly turn. The observance of propriety, doing and saying the correct thing, is esteemed one of the cardinal virtues. It is the fruit of age-long saturation in the ethics of Confucians, which have added so much that is good to the national character. Propriety oils the wheels of social intercourse. This I found was to my advantage on many occasions. Candour, however, compels me to add that this decorum was, for the most part, but a superficial veneer, and afforded no true indication of what lay beneath the surface.

One could not be long resident among the Chinese without reflecting on their ant-like industry. This is particularly observable in the poorer sections of society, which indeed make up the bulk of the people. The main reason for this plodding diligence of the masses is to be found in their extreme poverty. The struggle is literally a struggle for bare existence. Small wonder then that an insatiable craving for money is a prevailing obsession, for money spells life. Times are very hard when harvests have been bad, and the price of rice has risen steeply. But there are easier times, too, when the crops have been good; and this is reflected in relaxed tension and happier faces. With reference to the most prosperous days there is an enlightening passage in The Sacred Edict describing the height of family bliss as 'having the mouth full of rice, slapping the belly, and laughing'.

But the scramble for hard cash is not confined to the poor. It is the eager pursuit of all classes; from the highest official to the humblest coolie. The love of money is an outstanding component in the makeup of the Chinese character.

Closely linked with industry, and the struggle to obtain the means of livelihood, is the most meticulous economy. Not a particle of food, not a grain of rice, is wasted. The domestic animals are consequently very badly off and have to fend for themselves. The dogs, pigs, and chickens, become the scavengers and pick up what scrap of garbage they can glean from the courtyards and streets.

It has been observed that a Chinese dog will never look up to its master, or to anyone else, for a modicum of food, knowing quite well that nothing is to be expected by way of voluntary offers from human beings. Their eyes and noses are always on the ground searching for morsels that may have inadvertently fallen, or for refuse too decayed for human consumption.

Another failure which is sure to be quickly observed by the foreigner is the Chinese disregard of time. With all their patient industry, there was no hurry. The hours of work were the hours of daylight, from dawn to sun-down. The time of day was immaterial, and there was no scramble to get a job done by a certain hour. The work could always be resumed on the morrow, so why hustle? As their own proverb has it, 'Min t'ien hai yio ih t'ien' – There is still another day tomorrow.

The persevering labour of which I have spoken applies particularly to the bread-winning common people. It was far otherwise with the well-to-do, whose circumstances placed them beyond the reach of anxiety, and who appeared to find too little to occupy their time.

Indolence and self-indulgence resulted in physical inertia and great reluctance to undertake anything which meant bodily exertion. There was a total lack of healthy open-air sports, nothing took the place of our cricket, football, tennis, and other out-door games. No-one took exercise of any kind for the sake of exercise. They preferred to sit about, sip tea, and eat melon seeds or peanuts. Lack of exercise and over-eating resulted in obesity, kidney troubles, and dyspepsia.

This torpidity of body was matched by a corresponding passivity of mind. There was very little trace of any intensive study of anything. The scholars conned the old faded classics of Confucius and Mencius; but they made little effort to add anything new themselves. They apparently took the view that the last words of wisdom had long ago been uttered, and that for them to presume to contribute any reflections of their own would be an impertinence. Nor did the literati exert themselves to add anything to history or biography. Original intellectual effort seemed paralysed under the spell of the past: and though brains and ability were not lacking, they were not employed; they appeared to be held, as it were, in a state of suspended animation.

Aversion to any kind of change (even where change would make for a greater ease and convenience) was obvious in the low standard of comfort which was tolerated. The houses were built of poor quality brick, and badly constructed. Permanent dampness was ensured by inadequate foundations and mud floors. The doors and paper windows were ill-fitting. There were no fireplaces, or any method of interior heating, except the charcoal brazier. In the winter the inmates depended for warmth on their thick padded garments; more and more being super-added as the weather got colder. There was no water laid on; every drop had to be hoisted up from the well, or brought in buckets from the river. There were no bath-rooms. At night a dim light was provided by paper lanterns, or small lamps burning an evil-smelling oil. Sanitation was of the most primitive kind. The furniture within the house was severe and uncomfortable, being innocent of all upholstery; the straight-backed chairs being particularly uneasy.

In addition there was the overcrowding, the lack of privacy, the noises within and without. All this, however, was what the people were accustomed to, and it was accepted as matter of course. They did not miss, because they had never known, the luxury of a quiet room, the warmth of an open fire, a cosy arm-chair, a warm bath, and a spring bed-stead. Consequently they accepted their hard life with cheerfulness. They appeared quite contented with their lot, and I never heard them complain.

Hardship has done much to mould the character of the Chinese people. It has developed in them a wonderful power of endurance. Even in times of great misfortune, when homes are broken up, and there is widespread destruction, they evince an uncomplaining fortitude that excites the sincerest admiration. Good-nature, cheerfulness, contentment, patience, and perseverance are surely sterling qualities in a people so subject to recurring disaster and so oppressed by poverty.

In China the younger generation is always in bondage to the elder; and each succeeding generation makes the same tedious demands. The small children are natural enough, and are frequently 'spoilt', but as they grow older 'propriety' requires of them more and more filial piety. This outward show of reverence for your parents and for your ancestors is the 'done' thing. Not to conform to the prescribed rites would be the height of 'bad form', and would involve a disgraceful 'loss of face'. It is shown in a variety of ways; more particularly when the parents are dying, or are dead. The provision of a specially fine coffin, made of the best wood and heavily lacquered, which the parents may view in the sick room before they make their final congé, will be an act particularly gratifying to their hearts. Then there must follow an impressive funeral procession, and proper observance of the rules of mourning. Some will not infrequently sell up their all, even to the house timbers if necessary in order to provide fitting obsequies for the deceased.

Filial piety requires also the periodic observance of the ceremonies connected with ancestral worship: in itself a wearisome bondage. On anniversary days food is offered, and the obeisance is made, before the tablets on which the names of the departed ones are inscribed. This takes place in the central hall of the ancestral home. At the grave side imitation paper money is burnt to provide for their necessities in the other world. Sometimes a vacant place is left at table and food is placed before the empty chair, while such observations are made as 'Grandfather, please eat'. In these ways the spirits must be appeased. They must be shown that those left behind remember them. If they are neglected they will be displeased and may bring trouble on the family.

Religious sentiment is strong in the Chinese, although their groping after the super-natural is pitifully confused. They take for granted the survival of the human spirit. Spirits are everywhere. There are the good spirits, as of one's own ancestry, which must be appeased and kept in good humour; and there are the bad spirits, which must be propitiated, or deceived, or frightened away. Consequently pilgrimages, offerings at the grave-side, oblations and prostrations, the burning of incense, and the discharge of fire-crackers, figure largely in their religious observances.

Confucianism is often referred to as a 'religion', but it cannot rightly be so regarded. It is more in the nature of the ethical code. It must be conceded that the sayings of the ancients which have been preserved and which comprise The Chinese Classics, set a high standard of morality. They uphold a lofty ideal of personal conduct, and this ideal, kept constantly before the people, has undoubtedly exerted great influence for good upon the nation as a whole. The Classics are revered by all, and the high principles which they inculcate are approved; although that is very far from saying that they are universally put into practice.

I suppose the religion that can claim the largest number of adherents is Buddhism, but it exists, so far as I have observed it, in a very corrupt form. Buddhist temples are to be found in every city, 'joss-houses' in every village, and shrines by every road-side. Priests – in their long grey gowns, and with their shaven heads – one meets with everywhere. In the aggregate they constitute a vast unwashed multitude. What I saw of them was not prepossessing. Their lazy life does not conduce to personal cleanliness or to moral integrity. They are regarded with contempt by the people, who yet defer to them as the exponents of 'religion'. A curious paradox. The trouble is that religion and morality are considered as two entirely separate things and completely divorced the one from the other. Morality is not held to be an integral part of religion; I speak not of Buddhism in its theoretic conceptions, but as exemplified in its living votaries, and as I observed it in the personnel of the priesthood. What matters is temple attendance, prayers and sacrifices to the idols, and the practice of the outward forms of pious ritual. As the smoke of incense ascends the worshippers kneel on the temple floor with heads bowed low, repeating the invocation of the priest, 'O-mi-do-Fu'(Oh Buddha, Oh Buddha); each repetition punctuated by bumping the head to the ground, and by the rhythmic beat of the drum. Prayers will also be made to Kwan-yin-pu-Sah (Goddess of Mercy), the idol with the hundred arms outstretched to help suffering women.

There is also the worship of Nature. Temples are dedicated to the sun and the moon; to the gods of the wind and of thunder. The tall trees which grow around the temples are held in special reverence as they are thought to embody the temple spirits. Certain animals, too, are revered, such as the hedge-hog, the rat, and the snake. The water-snake is held to be an embodiment of the spirit of the floods. When the floods break out the snake is worshipped, and prayers are made to it for the subsidence of the waters. If they subside there are great celebrations in honour of the snake, specimens of which are captured and exhibited in the temples – where the people may go and pay homage. Even the officials will go and prostrate themselves before this 'god', whether they share the popular belief or not. It is expected of them and they feel bound to observe the time-honoured ceremonies.

There are many other gods. There is the domestic or kitchen god, who, at the close of each year, ascends to heaven to report on the behaviour of the family. As it is of the utmost importance that he should give a 'good conduct report', the lips of his wooden effigy are smeared with soft candy. This will sweeten his words and ensure that only nice things are reported! It is strange that an intelligent race like the Chinese should entertain such childish ideas and should think that they can so easily out-wit the gods; which, at the same time, they hold in such dread, and consider to be so potent for evil. It is quite common for a small boy to be dressed in a girl's clothes, or be given a girl's name. In this the evil spirits will be deceived and not do him any harm. They would not consider a girl worth bothering about!

Such was the thick darkness in which the people groped. Their degenerate priesthood, and their decayed shrines and temples, were symbolic of spiritual ruin. But China's mental attitude was such that she would not have admitted depravity in any form, and would have scorned the idea that she was in any need of help or enlightenment from the despised nations of the West. But whether she liked it or not, help from without was imperative – friendly and sympathetic help; the rejuvenation which comes from the influx of new ideas, new realms of learning, enlightened religious faith. Buddha and Confucius had shed their limited light for wayfaring men; but after the Sun had arisen there is no further need for candles.

# Chapter X

# HISTORICAL AND POLITICAL

I have attempted in the preceding chapter to give some idea of the more obvious traits in Chinese life which early drew my attention. And the first thing that I mentioned, because it obtruded itself so painfully, was the deep-rooted sentiment of antipathy which existed towards the foreigner. I was bound in consequence to lead a secluded life, and my time, as already indicated, was spent mainly in study. The waiting time before I could open my doors and engage in medical work with any prospect of success seemed very long. Owing to my unpopularity as a 'barbarian', and to the general unrest, it was destined to be even longer than I anticipated. I feel it is necessary to an intelligent understanding of my circumstances at this time that I should give my reader some account of the disturbed political state of the country.

The exclusive attitude of the Chinese towards foreigners was no new thing; it had been the national posture for centuries. The successive dynasties (if I may here introduce a brief historical note) extending back some 2,000 years B.C. had maintained the same tradition. Outside nations were rigorously shut out.[18] This may have arisen from the constantly recurring necessity of having to resist aggression. We read of the Great Wall being repaired and strengthened as early as 220 B.C. But resistance was not always successful. The Mongols invaded China under Genghis Khan early in the 13th century; and in 1280 A.D.

18 [FW] Dr Peake oversimplifies: the Great Wall was never quite the sort of barrier that Europeans believed (see Julia Lovell, *The Great Wall: China Against the World 1000 BC–AD 2000*, London, 2006) and during the Tang Dynasty (AD 618–907), for example, the Chinese capital was the largest and most cosmopolitan city in the world, with Sogdian merchants, Manichaean and Nestorian Christian temples, and mosques.

Kublai Khan became Emperor of the whole of China, founding the Mongol Dynasty, which lasted from 1280 to 1368. The war-like Kublai extended his conquests to the very frontiers of Europe. He seems to have been broader-minded than his successors, for under his rule not only were outsiders tolerated, but many foreign adventurers (including Marco Polo) were made welcome at his magnificent Court. The Mongol Dynasty was succeeded by the Ming, 1368–1644, during which the capital was moved from Nanking to Peking.

Then in 1644 came another foreign invasion, this time from Manchuria. The Manchu numbered some 3,000,000, and the Chinese something like 200,000,000; but being a hardy, warlike race they made an easy conquest over the more passive Chinese. The Manchu, or Ta Ching [Qing], Dynasty persisted until early in the present century (1912). Under its first two Emperors, K'ang-Hsi and Chien-Lung [Kangxi, Qianlong], the wide Empire extended over Manchuria, Mongolia, China, Tibet, and Turkistan – and China reached her zenith of cultural development. As time went on the Chinese, being in such numerical superiority, gradually absorbed the Manchus, who by degrees lost their former martial qualities and slowly degenerated. Sporadic rebellion against the Ruling House broke out from time to time. The Empress-Dowager, Her Majesty Tsu-Hsi [Cixi], in her resolute and spirited reign, may be regarded as the last spark of the slowly dying fire. The last rebellion, that of 1911, brought the Manchu Dynasty, and the age-long monarchical system of government, to a close.

When I reached China towards the end of the last century, His Majesty, the Emperor Kwang-Hsu [Guangxu], had recently been forced to vacate his rightful place on the Dragon Throne. He was the nephew of the Empress-Dowager. During his minority the Regency had devolved upon his august Aunt, but on his attaining his majority at the age of 19 he took up the reins of government, and Tsu-Hsi, who was popularly known as 'The Old Buddha', found time to enjoy the deights of her Summer Palace outside Peking; though, from time to time, she still interfered in the affairs of state.[19]

---

19  [FW] The Dowager Empress Tsu-Hsi (Cixi, 1835–1908) was a concubine of the Hsien-feng (Xianfeng) Emperor (r. 1850–61) and bore his only son, the T'ung-chih (Tongzhi) Emperor (r. 1862–75). On her son's death, she placed a nephew on the

*An aristocratic Manchu lady (right).*
*Postcard from Dr Peake's collection.*

In the year 1898 the Emperor was 28 years of age, a progressive but dissatisfied young man. In marked contrast to the prevailing sentiments of the nation he deplored the backwardness of his country as compared with Western lands, of which he had an intelligent understanding. His great ambition was to inaugurate far-reaching measures of Reform, and to usher in a new era of enlightened progress.

The Old Buddha, on the other hand, entertained no such notions. She was a quick-witted, energetic woman of marked natural abilities, but having originally been the No. 1 Concubine of the late Emperor Hsien-Fung [Xianfeng], chosen from the homes of the people like other Manchu girls, and sequestered as she was within the walls of the Forbidden City, she was profoundly ignorant of the rest of the world, and, in her arrogant self-esteem, regarded the foreigner with the utmost contempt and detestation. She was emphatically of 'the old school', viewing with abhorrence anything in the nature of change, or of new ideas imported from without; more particularly if such innovations were calculated to affect the time-honoured usage and routine of the Court. Opinions so diametrically opposed as those held by the Empress-Dowager and her Imperial nephew could not but lead to trouble.

The imposing gate-ways leading through the high containing walls of the Forbidden City (an enclosed domain within Peking itself, and commonly referred to by both Manchus and Chinese as 'The Great Within') are closely guarded. All entrance was forbidden, except to high Ministers of State obeying commands to Throne Audiences, or to Imperial Tutors and Physicians; and of necessity to messengers, eunuchs, and Court servants on their lawful business.

'The Great Within' represented the absolute authority and sovereignty of the state, the nerve-centre of autocratic government, where the old Buddha ruled supreme; it also featured a depraved medieval court, functioning exactly as it had done for many centuries. The Imperial Concubines numbered many hundreds, most of whom were probably quite unknown to the Emperor; and on the Palace staff were literally thousands of court officials, eunuchs, and female servants. The

---

throne, the Kuang-Hsu Emperor, and effectively ruled herself from 1875 to 1908.

100

life of boredom, jealousy, and intrigue which was the lot of these unfortunate dependents was a not infrequent cause of suicide. It was from her favourite eunuchs, acting as spies, that the Old Buddha obtained her information as to all that was going on within the palaces. These servile creatures were unscrupulous, rapacious, and cruel. But their rapacity and cruelty were more than matched by the despotic and vengeful woman who held the reins of tyranny so firmly in her grasp.

It was in the summer of 1898 (the Dowager being absent at the Summer Palace) that the Emperor felt the time had come to launch his Reform scheme. The inspiring leader of the 'Reform Movement' was in reality K'ang Yu-wei [Kang Youwei],[20] who hailed from the southern province of Canton.

He came that year to Peking, and was invited to secret conferences with His Majesty. They discussed together the remedial measures which were most urgently needed, particularly those relating to education, representative government, military reorganisation and so on; probably also the steps to be taken to clean up the Augean Stables at the centre, i.e. in the Forbidden City itself. Together they found a similarity of views, and a natural affinity of spirit, which was most heartening to them both.

The Emperor entered into the scheme for the betterment of his country with the greatest enthusiasm; and with K'ang's assistance a series of Proclamations was drawn up. But he was not unaware that bitter antagonism would be aroused. The ultra-conservative mandarins would range themselves in deadly opposition, but the one most to be feared was the Old Buddha herself. It was probably because of this that the Reform Edicts were promulgated in such rapid succession. The idea, evidently, was to rush the reforms through before the reactionary elements had recovered their balance and had had time to mature their plans of resistance. At the same time the Emperor knew quite well how dangerous was the venture upon which he had embarked, especially as the elimination of the Dowager was essential to success.

---

20 [FW] K'ang Yu-wei (Kang Youwei, 1858–1927), a scholar who helped the Kwang-hsu Emperor to launch a major series of reforms in 1898 which were soon stopped by the Dowager-Empress. K'ang Yu-wei continued to press for a constitutional monarchy.

He felt the need of powerful support. To whom should he turn? He decided to confide in H.E. Yuan Shi-K'ai [Yuan Shikai],[21] a very able official, who also had the necessary military strength at his disposal. He seemed to be the very man. In a secret interview His Majesty and Yuan worked out the conspiracy in full detail, which included the arrest and close custody of the Old Buddha. Yuan consented to put the plot into execution. But the traitor straightaway betrayed his trust: and divulged the whole scheme to H.E. Jung-lu [Ronglu],[22] who was Commander-in-Chief of the army, a Grand Councillor, and a kinsman of Her Majesty; a man who then and always remained her staunch friend and faithful protector. Jung-Lu repaired immediately to the Summer Palace and there disclosed the intrigue. The irate Dowager, blazing with indignation, hastened at once to her palace in the Forbidden City where she demanded the immediate attendance of the unfortunate Kuang-Hsu. She therefore accused him of the conspiracy, and her knowledge and detail showed him only too plainly that he had been basely betrayed. He was completely in her power and could only fall on his knees at her feet, but was instantly put under arrest and conveyed as a prisoner to a small island in one of the lakes of the palace grounds. Here he was kept under strict guard in a small pavilion; never leaving his prison except to be escorted periodically to the palace, there to prostrate himself before his vindictive Aunt. This she ordained that she might assure herself of his proper subservience and to gloat over his subjection and misery. Misery was indeed his lot. The Empress, his wife, a pliable woman who had been chosen for him by the Dowager that she might act as a 'go-between 'and spy, sided with the Old Buddha. His one true friend was the 'Pearl Concubine', and she was torn from him and confined within the palace precincts. Fifty-three of the eunuchs who had been

---

21 [FW] A general who rose to considerable power as the Dowager Empress attempted rather tardily to modernise the Imperial armies and, after the establishment of the Republic of China in 1912, sought personal power as president, dissolving parliament in 1914. His attempt to establish himself as a new Emperor was ended by his death.
22 [FW] Jung-lu (Ronglu, 1836–1903) was a Manchu official who held high office in the Imperial Household and the Peking Gendarmerie and who was trusted by the Dowager-Empress.

faithful servants to him were beaten to death. They were replaced by a few others who could be trusted to report his every word and action. He was left without a friend.

Tsu-Hsi then issued an Edict in the name of the Emperor in which he was made to say that he was fully aware of his hopeless incompetence, that he was unequal to the duties which as Head of the State devolved upon him, and that he had implored Her Imperial Majesty the Empress-Dowager, who had so brilliantly guided the affairs of State in the days of his minority, again to take over the onerous task of government. To this Her Majesty had graciously condescended to give her consent!

Having resumed the Regency the Old Buddha's first care was to cancel all the Reform Edicts. She then laid her plans for Kuang-Hsu's early demise. Very mysteriously he fell sick, and a proclamation was issued notifying the people that the Emperor was gravely ill. For the sake of appearances the most famous physicians were summoned from the Provinces to attend him. But this 'sickness' was fully understood by the people, and they knew that foul play was afoot. The arrival of the physicians was also thoroughly appreciated. This was only to be expected in order to 'save face'.

Perhaps the most famous of these physicians was Chen Ling-fang, a man over 70 years of age, who came from the southern city of Soo-chow [Suzhou]. When summoned into the Imperial Presence, etiquette required of this old man that he should cross the floor of the Audience Hall on his knees, and remain in that posture, with his eyes fixed on the ground, throughout the interview. He was not required to ask any questions, and there was nothing in the nature of an examination. All that the physician was allowed to do was to place his fingers on the wrists of his illustrious patient. The doctor was then permitted to retire.

He then reported his diagnosis, and recommendations for treatment, to the Grand Council, who later acquainted the Throne regarding his opinion. Realising the Emperor's depressed state of health, both physically and mentally, it is not surprising that he prescribed tonic and complete rest of mind and body. I have mentioned this incident of professional attendance on His Majesty as it will serve to illustrate how the practice of medicine was carried on even in China's most exalted quarters.

In Peking, and in the North generally, the intrigues of the Palace were accepted, with a shrug of the shoulders, as being in accord with the annals of the Great Within; but the whole foul and treacherous drama was differently viewed in the South. The Southern provinces, and particularly the Cantonese, were now clamant for reform; and the frustrations of the Emperor's programme had set them seething with discontent. They were on the verge of rebellion. Their avowed object was to sweep away Manchu despotism and substitute a Republican form of government. Their leaders were Sun Yat-sen and K'ang Yu-wei, both of whom had had to flee from the wrath of the Old Buddha with a price upon their heads. Some of the leading Reformers, and many of the rank and file, had been seized and ruthlessly executed at the command of the Dowager. Decapitated heads were put into cages, and distributed about the country as a warning to others. I myself, in Hunan, saw one hoisted on the top of a pole. It had been forwarded from Wuchang and was conspicuously displayed in the open street.

Only a match was required to set the tinder ablaze. The death of the Emperor would supply it. His murder would furnish the rallying cry for open rebellion of the South against the North. The Old Buddha was well aware of this, and she was worried. Memorials from the Provinces, and even from such highly placed Mandarins as the Viceroy of Nanking, poured into the Forbidden City, and warned her, no doubt in very guarded language, that if the Emperor were to die the Southern pot would boil over. She hesitated. A brake was put upon the criminal means which were in operation against His Majesty's life. He slowly began to improve and in a few weeks' time had fully recovered. The storm which had threatened died down, and the danger to the Throne was averted.

But from henceforth to the end the Emperor remained a lonely, heart-stricken, and bitterly disappointed man; an Emperor only in name, a nonentity, a prisoner, stripped of all dignity and authority. To such a miserable and humiliating pass was the 'Son of Heaven', the 'Lord of Ten Thousand Years', reduced. His tragic and pitiable reign is surely unparalleled in the age-long history of his Imperial ancestry!

# Chapter XI

# THE BOXER RISING

The Empress-Dowager was again firmly in the saddle, holding the reins with a closer hand than ever. She would have no nonsense from these pestilent Reformers. She would reign as sole Dictator. There was the Grand Council, composed of the Princes and the highest Ministers of State, it is true; but the Council only met when she called it, and its function was purely advisory.

The Grand Council Audiences were held in the special 'Audience Hall'. The Councillors were ushered into the Presence on their knees, kow-towing with heads to the floor as they advanced, and they remained on their knees throughout the audience. A curtain was suspended before the Throne. Thus the august and sacred Person of Her Majesty was screened from the vulgar eyes of even the most exalted of her subjects. At one side of the screen stood her favourite eunuch, Li Lianying.[23] In this position he was able to observe every indication of the will of his Mistress (whom he adored) and also to peer round the edge and see that the demeanour of the Councillors was consistent with their proper subservience. As to procedure, Her Majesty would introduce the matter that happened to be on her mind, and then each of her Advisers would in turn express his opinion. The Dowager, having heard their different points of view, would dismiss the Council, and then make her own decisions.

After the collapse of the Emperor's Reform schemes, and while there was still much discontent in the country in consequence, Tsu-Hsi sought to turn the attention of the people to some other national

---

23 [FW] Li Lianying, 1848–1911, the most important eunuch in the Forbidden City.

grievance, and thus to ensure that all danger of rebellion had been eliminated. She found it ready to her hand in the universal hostility which existed towards the foreigners; and now, most opportunely, a movement was afoot which would distract the thoughts of the malcontents and concentrate hatred on the foreign devils.

The Movement, which originated in the north-eastern province of Shantung [Shandong], was known as 'the Boxer Rising'. It had as its sole objective the extermination of the foreigner. Internal questions were shelved, and in their place, from the Dragon Throne downwards, to wipe out the barbarians from over-seas by wholesale massacre became the dominant theme. Excitement, and rumours relative to our imminent annihilation, spread through the provinces like a prairie fire. The foreign devil was responsible for the droughts and famine, the floods and epidemics, which afflicted the country with such unfailing regularity. There could be no prosperity so long as a single barbarian remained within the borders of the Middle Kingdom.

Away in distant Hunan there was an exacerbation of animosity towards us. Many rumours were current as to our reasons for taking up residence within the Province. That we had ulterior motives was taken for granted. As to my 'doctoring', that was merely a pretext, and any people mad enough to entrust themselves to my care would certainly be 'bewitched'. Was it not a fact that foreigners ate the hearts and livers of Chinese babies; and that foreign doctors gouged out their eyes to make their medicines? It would be unprofitable to relate the many ridiculous stories which were in circulation. If I appeared on the street I would be followed by an unfriendly crowd calling me opprobrious names. On one occasion, as I was being carried in my chair, a band of hooligans roistering down the street rounded a corner and was on us before we could make any attempt to evade them. My bearers promptly lowered the chair to one side, and one of them quickly dropped my front curtain. Fortunately I was not 'spotted', and the rabble swept on. That coolie's swift thought and action probably saved me from dire consequences.

The attitude of the populace became so hostile that the Tao-t'ai insisted on posting an armed guard in the vicinity of my premises – a careful watch was kept on my movements, and if I appeared outside, the guard would immediately turn out, fall in behind, and follow. In these circumstances it would have been foolish, and only asking for trouble, to attempt to do anything in the way of medical work.

To go back to the Boxers (or 'Pugilists') who were immediately responsible for this wide-spread recandescence of anti-foreign feeling. Who were they? Originally they were just gangs of hot-heads; young fellows lacking sufficient occupation, who, under the euphemistic title of 'the Plum Blossom Fists', banded themselves together with the avowed object of exterminating the foreign devil. This was in 1899, the year following the collapse of the Emperor's Reform Movement, but it had nothing to do with that ill-fated scheme. It was frankly anti-foreign. Intense fanaticism, and fantastic ignorance, were the outstanding characteristics of the Boxers; but they were actuated too, at least in part, by a crude patriotism, for had not the outer barbarians encroached upon their country's territory? Only recently, in their own province of Shantung, the sacred birth province of Confucius, Germany had seized the port of Kiao-chou [Jiaozhou] and adjoining hinterland.[24]

The Rising was at first frowned upon by the authorities and could very easily have been crushed but as it grew in strength it grew in favour. Many regarded it as the Heaven-sent means of China's deliverance. The difference of opinion among leading mandarins was the cause of a vacillating policy which allowed the movement to gather momentum. The notorious and blood-thirsty Governor of Shantung, Yu-hsien [Yuxian],[25] whole-heartedly supported it, and wrote of it in eulogistic terms to the Empress-Dowager, recommending her

---

24 [ECP] Germany had enforced the 'lease' of the port of Kiao-chou, with its adjacent territory, under the pretext of 'compensation' for the murder of two of her missionaries.
25 [FW] Governor of Shandong, where the Boxer movement began as an anti-dynastic rebellion, partly the result of a terrible drought in the area. He was famously anti-foreign and may have helped to steer the Boxers away from their anti-dynastic views towards anti-foreign activities. He was moved to Taiyuan where the worst massacre of foreign missionaries and their families took place in 1900. He was reported as having tried to commit suicide by eating gold in 1901 but, having recovered, he was executed in the same year as part of the reparation demanded by the foreign powers at the end of the Boxer uprising.

encouragement. She was not slow in taking his advice. On these two, the Old Buddha and her brutal henchman Yu-hsien, the responsibility for the ghastly tragedy of the Boxer atrocities mainly rests.

The 'Fists', in their separate localities, met daily for their 'drills', which were more in the nature of gymnastic antics than anything else. Brandishing their weapons, and uttering blood-curdling yells, they would spring at one another in frenzied encounter. Intense fanaticism was of the essence of the cult; the more extreme working themselves into a madness, acting wildly, foaming at the mouth and falling into trances. Charms and incantations figured prominently.

The most important of these charms consisted merely of a small piece of yellow paper on which a grotesque figure was drawn in vermillion ink, with the characters for Buddha, Tiger, and Dragon. Fearful and wonderful were the magic arts and rites accompanying the ceremonies of initiation. True Boxers, properly initiated, and wearing the charm, believed themselves immune to sword thrusts and rifle bullets, which, passing through their bodies, would leave them unharmed. They claimed to be endowed with a 'divine mission of retaliation', and when on the march they carried huge banners inscribed 'The gods assist us to destroy all foreigners'.

By the year 1900 the Movement reached quite alarming proportions in the northern provinces, invading Peking itself in the early half of the year. Owing to the favourable attitude adopted by the Dowager and some of her high Manchu officials towards the Boxers it was exceedingly difficult for the military to deal with the situation. Her Majesty's Grand Secretary and Commander-in-Chief of the imperial troops, Jung-lu, on whom she was accustomed to rely, strongly advised her to have the Rising suppressed and the leaders arrested and executed. He ridiculed their pretensions to a 'divine mission', and their claims of invulnerability to swords and bullets. He well knew that the course events were taking would deeply embroil the country with the Foreign Powers. Unfortunately his advice was over-ridden by that of the majority in an Audience of the Grand Council. The Old Buddha sided with the majority. Not only so, but where, here and there, an official had attempted to curb Boxer excesses, she had him cashiered and degraded. Under such conditions how was it possible to suppress the Rising?

When the Boxer hordes ran amok in Peking urgent instructions were dispatched by the British Minister to the foreign residents to take refuge within the protecting walls of the British Legation. Not all succeeded in reaching this place of sanctuary in time. The first foreigner to be murdered was the Japanese interpreter attached to the Japanese Legation. Then Professor James of the Imperial University was caught in the street, prodded with bayonets, and later decapitated, his head being exposed in a cage at one of the main gates. There was also the German Minister, Baron von Ketteler, who was shot in the street while being carried in his sedan-chair.

The city was in an uproar. Churches and foreign houses were looted and set on fire. The lives and property of Christian converts, known as 'secondary devils', did not escape. Thousands were slain. Many others were killed on mere suspicion, and without proof that they were in any way connected with foreigners. Even little children were butchered.

Encouraged by the success of this armed rabble in slaughtering 16,000 native Christians and a few defenceless foreigners, the Old Buddha issued a Proclamation, which ran as follows:

Now that all foreign churches and chapels have been razed to the ground, and no place of concealment is left for the foreigners, they must inevitably scatter, flying in every direction. Be it therefore known and announced to all men, that any person found guilty of harbouring foreigners will incur the penalty of decapitation. For every male foreigner taken alive a reward of 50 taels will be given, for every female 40 taels, and for every child 30 taels; but it is clearly to be understood that they shall be taken alive, and that they shall be genuine foreigners. Once this fact has been authenticated the reward will be paid without delay.
A Special Proclamation; requiring reverent obedience.

Outside Peking the same relentless policy of hate was being enacted. Yu-hsien, the former Governor of Shantung, but now transferred to

Shansi, memorialised the Throne seeking instructions with regard to the missionaries within his province. The reply of the Dowager was swift and unequivocal. 'I command', so ran her message, despatched by her fastest riders, 'that all foreigners – men, women, and children, old and young – be summarily executed. Let not one escape, so that my Empire may be purged of this noisome source of corruption, and that peace may be restored to my loyal subjects'. This was duly carried out. The missionaries and their children having been rounded up were herded into the courtyard of the Governor's Yamen at Tai-yuan-fu, the capital of the province, and brutally massacred by decapitation; Yu-hsien himself participating in the bloody work. The future was to bring retribution.

The murder of foreign missionaries and their converts was accounted a comparatively unimportant matter by the Princes and Councillors about her Majesty; but when it came to attacking the accredited Ministers of the Great Powers within the Legation Quarters, there were those who showed signs of alarm. Jung-Lu, the Grand Secretary, as we have seen, deprecated the course being taken by the Dowager, but was over-ruled. The Emperor doubtless disapproved, but his opinions counted for nothing. The Old Buddha was determined; and thus encouraged, the Boxers laid siege to the British Legation, behind whose walls some hundreds of foreigners of different nationalities had taken refuge.

An Edict was now promulgated by the Dowager ordering the extermination of every foreigner within the realms. By some of the more enlightened officials the command was received with embarrassment. In all fairness it should be recorded that there *were* those to whom the cruel and senseless policy being pursued by the Old Buddha was entirely repugnant. In *China under the Empress-Dowager* Bland and Backhouse relate how two Peking Officials even dared to alter the wording of the Edict.[26] They changed the character for 'slay' to 'protect'.

---

26 [FW] Dr Peake seems to have relied considerably upon *China Under the Empress Dowager* by J. O. P. Bland and Edmund Trelawney Backhouse (London, 1910). Bland had served in the Chinese Imperial Customs Service and from 1896 to 1911 was *The Times* correspondent in Shanghai. He collaborated with Backhouse on the book, basing much of the content on the diary of a Chinese official which Backhouse

This was discovered and their decapitation ordered. Their names were Yuan and Hau. Just before the sword fell Yuan turned to his companion and said 'I hope that the sun may soon return to his right place in the heavens. We shall meet again at the Yellow Springs. To die is only to come home'. Such an act of humanity, and of courageous intervention on behalf of the despised foreigner, stands out in refreshing relief from the vindictive madness of those days.

So much for the events that were taking place in Peking. But in the South we did not escape. The extermination edict was disseminated throughout the length and breadth of the Empire. It was posted up in the streets. In Hunan, although the Decree was prominently displayed, as yet no action had been taken – the Governor awaiting confirmatory instructions from the Viceroy of the neighbouring provinces of Hupeh [Hubei]. Howbeit disturbing rumours filled the air, and the tension was growing.

Things were getting very uncomfortable in Heng-chow. Ah-shin was obviously in a state of acute nervous apprehension; and Chow-ling was glum, predicting the worst. He came to me one evening with a very gloomy countenance.

'May I have a few words with the doctor', he said.

'Yes, Chow-ling', I replied. 'What is it?'

'I have been on the streets', he explained, 'and heard the people talking. The outward signs are bad. Of course it is according to the doctor's wishes, but the way is still open. Dare I ask what are the doctor's intentions?'

'Chow-ling', I said, 'I have been thinking on the same lines as yourself. We must go while yet there is time'.

One night, soon afterwards, leaving the gate-keeper to lock up the premises, we made good our escape by water, and slipped rapidly down stream. Carried down on the swiftly flowing river the journey was a

---

had acquired. Backhouse has now been revealed as a terrific fraudster (cheating the University of Oxford, the British government and the American Bank Note company, amongst others), and the diary is now considered to be fraudulent as well. Offering an entirely negative view of the Dowager-Empress, it was very influential until doubts began to be cast upon the sources. See Hugh Trevor-Roper, *Hermit of Peking: The Hidden Life of Sir Edmund Backhouse*, London, 1993.

very much quicker one than it had been many months before when we had toiled up against the current. It now took days where formerly it had taken weeks. We reached the foreign settlement in Hankow safely, having encountered no trouble on the way. It was good to be amongst one's own people again, and to get all the news. They had been much concerned for our safety.

Hankow was in a state of suppressed excitement. The Edict had of course reached the city, and already, foreign property had been attacked and destroyed. Much depended on the attitude of the Viceroy, who resided in Wuchang, just across the river. What would he do? Would he dare to disobey the Imperial Mandate? He was notoriously a time-server and an opportunist. His great idea was always to be on the safe side. Had he thought that the foreigners could be permanently eliminated I do not think there can be any doubt as to what our fate would have been. But he had more sense than men like Yu-hsien. He knew that a foreign force was being hurried forward from the coast to the relief of the Peking Legation. He knew also something of the might of the Western Powers and feared that stern retribution would follow China's midsummer madness. He hesitated, holding the wilder elements in check. It was a mercy, for we could not have defended ourselves against the fury of a countless mob. We had no Legation within whose stout walls we could take refuge. It was reported, but I know not with what accuracy, that an express messenger had been despatched to H.E. the Viceroy to warn him that on the receipt of news of an attack being made on any of the foreign residents, the first shots from the *Woodcock*, a British gun-boat anchored in the river, would crash into his Yamen. In the meantime the ship's guns would be kept trained on the target.

The strain became very great. Our women and children, and those men who had no special reason for remaining, were all evacuated down river to Shanghai, and from thence across to Japan. One of the women, before leaving, said it would be a comfort to her if I would stay by her husband. He was not aware of her request. As he was stationed in Wuchang this necessitated my crossing to the other side. Things were decidedly hotter in Wuchang; and we felt completely cut off from all help, the river being a mile wide at this point. Moreover a great wall surrounds the city. The gates were closed every evening at sun-down, making all entrance or exit impossible. Thus at night we were completely trapped.

As our house happened to be quite close to the wall I mounted to the top of it one evening to reconnoitre, and discovered a spot on the battlements where I thought it might be possible to secure the end of a long rope, and so by this means lower ourselves down the outside to the ground. To escape unseen from a howling rabble surrounding the house would have been the difficulty, and our chance of so doing was a very slender one. But it gave me some plan of action which might be attempted, and for this purpose I kept a coiled rope under my bed ready for use should the emergency arise.

The summer of 1900 was a particularly hot one – the temperature rising sometimes over 100°F. Owing to the protracted drought the harvest prospects were unusually bad, and the people were restless and irritable. Everything conspired to aggravate the general unrest and to increase hostility against the foreigner.

As the tension grew more and more acute we kept as much as possible within our compound. But our servants, frequenting the tea-shops, were able to pick up the gossip and report to us. More than once, according to rumours, the night was fixed on which our houses were to be set on fire; but each appointed time came and passed without incident. One evening a messenger arrived in hot haste from Hankow urging our immediate return. More foreign property had been attacked and the British Consul had reason to fear imminent violence. There was just time to get through the gates before they closed. I thought it would be wise to take advice and go, but my colleague declined to move. That immobilised us both. However, whatever outrage was brewing it did not materialise.

In Hankow, foreign and native refugees (chiefly missionaries and converts) were arriving almost daily from inland towns and country districts. Numbers were sick, and others had been terribly knocked about. Many were the stories of narrow escapes – hiding in lofts, in grain-baskets, and even in cesspits – while mobs in search of them yelled, 'Kill the foreign devils'. Some had come hundreds of miles, concealing themselves in the tall millet or in the main crops during the day-time, and travelling under the cover of night. Occasionally, in attending on them, I was detained in Hankow, and have memories of the long convoys reaching the city, man and beast exhausted and stumbling along in the darkness. Some were able to ride in rough palanquins, and others on mules and donkeys. But many were too ill and were carried full length in litters suspended between two mules harnessed tandem. For this purpose very long bamboo poles were used. In the middle these poles formed the sides of the litter or stretcher, and the ends, forming the shafts, were fixed to the sides of the animals in front and behind. A rough canopy was rigged up over the patient. This made a very effective ambulance. The resilience of the bamboo absorbed the bumps and shocks which otherwise would have meant torture on the rough stony tracks. The dogged muleteer trudged ahead and the sure-footed beasts followed him. These cases were evacuated down river as soon as possible.

Almost every day I crossed the water to attend these broken refugees, getting back again in the evening before the gates were closed. It would have been more sensible and more safe, had I been free to do so, to remain over on the Hankow side. To go through the native streets and to cross the river twice daily was fraught with personal danger, and it consumed much time. The people were in an ugly mood. Hostility was obvious in their looks, in their muttered imprecations, and in their general bearing. When I reached the river-side, it was not easy, even by the offer of enhanced pay, to find a boatman willing to row me over. The water was very high, as it always is in the summer-time, and the current very strong. This necessitated rowing up against the stream in order to strike the opposite bank at the right landing-place. On this account it might take as much as two hours to get over. Nor was the journey made in any comfort. Sitting in an open sampan, the heat, and the glare reflected from the water, were well-nigh insufferable, in spite of white cotton suit, sun-helmet, and smoked glasses.

Some of the cases I attended in Hankow were in a shocking condition. Almost all were suffering from dysentery, the result of having to subsist on infected food and impure water. One case remains vividly

114

in my mind, the case of a missionary who had escaped in an amazing manner out of the very hands of his captors. He, too, was a very sick man. Dysentery had reduced him to a state of extreme emaciation. In addition he was covered with severe burns. When caught he had been rolled in his bedding, paraffin had been thrown on him and then set alight. In spite of this he had struggled free and made a miraculous escape.

Coming home one evening through the narrow streets of Wuchang I passed a high mandarin being carried along in his elaborate chair. An armed guard escorted the great man, marching both before and behind the chair-bearers. All stared at me as they passed, and one of the soldiers venomously exclaimed, 'Sah t'a!' [Sha ta!] (i.e. 'kill him') . That he should dare to do so, un-rebuked, was a bad sign.

The uncertain attitude of the Viceroy, blowing now hot now cold, reflected the fluctuating policy of Peking. For there were times when even the Old Buddha, though eager for our total destruction, wavered. When confident of success attacks upon the Legation Enclosure would increase in ferocity. But at times fear would take possession of her. Supposing the claims of the Boxers to invulnerability and invincibility were unfounded after all! What if the avenging army of the Western barbarians, already marching on its way up from the coast, should defeat her armies in the field and succeed in reaching Peking, where would she be then?

Then thus haunted by misgivings the attacks would decrease in violence, or even cease for a short time. During one such lull in the fighting, which occurred in a spell of intense heat, she ordered ice, water-melons, and fresh vegetables to be taken to the poor foreigners! A cunning motive prompted this manoeuvre. In the event of things turning out badly after all, would this gesture not serve as proof that she had entertained nothing but compassion for the besieged, that the Boxers had got out of hand, and that she had been powerless to restrain them? Had she not, in their distress, sent fruit, and vegetables to the foreigners? Surely that would prove her innocence!

Could the besieged hold out? That was the agonising question; for upon the answer to that depended the fate of all of us. The Viceroy in Wuchang, and other officials, suspended action while they awaited the outcome. In the steaming heat of that awful summer in the Yang-tse valley the days dragged on. Scraps of news came through from time to time of the Allied Expeditionary Force (over 12,000 men, of different nationalities, organised from the coastal war-ships, and under the leadership of Admiral Seymour) brushing aside the resistance of the Imperial troops, and drawing nearer and nearer to Peking. Anxiously, day by day, we hungered for news. We knew that if the Relief forces could arrive in time to save the Legation the whole anti-foreign movement would collapse. It would mean the deliverance of us all; in the Capital and in the Provinces alike. Some of us had friends within those bravely defended walls, and we shuddered to think what their fate would be if the infuriated hordes succeeded in bursting through.

But the suspense was broken at last! It was on the 14th day of August, 1900, after a siege lasting two months, that the exciting news reached us that our gallant men had fought their way through to Peking – a distance of 100 miles from the coast – that they had gained entrance into the city by forcing the Water-gate, that the Legation had been relieved, and that all our people were safe. We learnt too, with grim satisfaction, that the Old Buddha had fled!

It was, of course, only after the siege had been raised that we heard any details. I will here state but a few of the bare facts, as the epic story has been so fully recorded by some of those who actually participated. The number of foreign civilians, men, women, and children, that had found refuge within the Legation Compound was 473. The Legation guards, mainly British and Japanese, numbered 400. In addition there were some 2,000 Chinese Christians who had been brought in by the missionaries. All were concentrated in the British Quarter as the other Legations had been burnt down. There was a fair amount of food to begin with, and the wells supplied sufficient water. The defence was skilfully organised, and under able leadership, most of the fighting being done by the British and the Japanese, reinforced by volunteers. The walls were loop-holed for rifle fire, and terrible execution was wrought upon the massed ranks of Boxers. Casualties there were also on our side. From time to time successful sorties were made upon the enemy. Towards the end food and ammunition were running low and had to

116

be rationed. All the 80 horses and mules had been killed and eaten; and the meal barrels were empty. From the heat and the over-crowding, from the stench of dead bodies, from hunger, and from anxiety, many were seriously ill, and all medical supplies were exhausted. Towards the end the Boxers were far advanced with their mining, by which means they intended to break into the compound from underground, and the situation was extremely critical. The native Christians dug trenches to counter-mine the enemy. Their active help all through the siege was invaluable. It has been admitted that the defence would have been impossible without the labour supplied by them.

The last attack, on the night of August the 12th, was made by the regular troops, as the Boxers were discredited. The attack was repelled; but two days later, when the defenders were at the end of their resources, they were overjoyed by the arrival of the Relief Force, and their terrible ordeal, borne with such heroic fortitude, was over.

大清國當今聖母皇太后萬歲萬歲萬萬歲

*The 'Old Buddha', Empress-Dowager Tsu-Hsi.*
*Postcard from Dr Peake's collection.*

# Chapter XII

# LAST YEARS OF THE EMPRESS-DOWAGER

It would be convenient here to anticipate the future and very briefly to record the subsequent history of the Empress-Dowager.

Before dawn on 14 August 1900, even while the Relief Expedition was forcing an entrance into the City, the Old Buddha made her hair-breadth escape from the Great Within. It was a humiliating experience for Tsu-Hsi. 'Alas, that it should come to this!' she is reported to have exclaimed when she beheld herself in the mirror disguised in the blue cotton garments of a peasant woman, with her hair dressed in the Chinese style and not in the elaborate head-dress of a Manchu lady.

There was great consternation and much hurry and scurry in the Palace, but the Old Buddha kept her nerve and showed no sign of panic. The Emperor's concubines, the female servants, and the eunuchs (with the exception of the Chief Eunuch, Li Lianying, and a few others) were summoned at 3.30 a.m. and ordered to remain behind, as it was necessary to reduce the numbers composing the retinue as much as possible. The Emperor, having nothing to fear from the foreigners, and anxious to escape the clutches of his spiteful Aunt, wished to remain behind, but this was denied him.[27]

It was then that the Pearl Concubine, throwing herself down at Her Majesty's feet, begged to be allowed to accompany the Emperor. She was sharply silenced. On venturing to renew her pleading she aroused

---

27 [ECP] Doubtless the Dowager feared that, under the aegis of the Western Powers, Kwang-Hsu would be restored to his rightful place on the Throne.

the wrath of the Old Buddha, who could tolerate no interference. Attending eunuchs were ordered to carry her off and throw her down the Palace Well. This cold-blooded and inhuman command was immediately carried out. The procession then formed up, passed through the Palace gates and, threading its way down the dark empty streets, passed through the north-western main gateway, and so on to the narrow track leading for hundreds of miles into the far interior.

Travelling in a common chair with no proper protection from the sun, putting up at night in inns of the meaner sort, subsisting on coarse food to which she was wholly unaccustomed, and brooding over her present plight and the loss of her Throne, the Old Buddha suffered severe physical discomfort and poignant mental anguish. She must now have realised how disastrously mistaken had been her anti-foreign policy, and how calamitous her support of the Boxers. The autocratic Dictator of the Celestial Empire was now a poorly-clad fugitive from the very aliens she had so despised and had attempted to exterminate.

A halt was called at Tai-yuan-fu [Taiyuan], the capital of the province of Shansi [Shanxi]. Here the Governor, Yu-hsien, warned by courier of the approach of Their Majesties, had made preparation for their reception. He had vacated his Yamen and placed it entirely at the disposal of the royal refugees. Here the Old Buddha extracted from the Governor every detail with regard to the massacre of the missionaries. She was taken into the courtyard to be shown the exact spot where the 57 missionaries and their children had been beheaded, shown the great two-handed sword which had been the instrument of their execution, heard how the Governor himself had taken a hand in the brutal work and evinced a positive relish in the circumstantial account attending the cruel murder of these innocent victims, whose only object in the country, at much personal sacrifice, was the good of her people. Yet they were upheld in their terrible ordeal by an Unseen Power. Chinese eye-witnesses have testified to the wonderful dignity and calm with which they faced their end.

From Tai-yuan-fu the fugitives journeyed on and finally came to rest at Hsi-an [Xi'an], in the province of Shensi [Shaanxi]. Here, 1,000 miles of rough road from Peking, the Old Buddha felt herself to be comparatively safe; and it was at this place she remained during the whole period of her exile. Here she set up her little Court; little as regards its entourage compared with Peking, but big as ever with regard to its greedy demands on the people. Poor as they were, and at however great a sacrifice, 'tribute' must flow into her coffers – silks – furs – jade – silver.

The Old Buddha sat tight at Hsi-an for over a year, biding her time, and keenly watching events from afar. Above all she was determined to lie low until the demands of the Foreign Powers had been finally formulated. What were to be the terms of settlement? Would she be required to abdicate and give place to the Emperor? Much foreign sentiment was in favour of such a course, and the Dowager was acutely apprehensive as to the trend events were taking in Peking. It was not until the terms of the Peace Protocol were promulgated, more than twelve months after the collapse of the Boxers, and she found that no retributive action was to be taken against herself, that the Old Buddha felt it safe to leave her distant retreat and to start on her return journey to the capital.

Though the Peace Terms did not touch Her Majesty personally, they did require – among other demands, such as the payment of substantial indemnities[28] – the execution, exile, or degradation of the Boxer leaders; and these she was powerless to save. It was a great mistake that the restoration of H.M. Kwang-Hsu to his rightful place on the Throne was not insisted upon. Had this been done the corrupt Court would have been cleansed, reforms introduced, and a Constitutional Monarchy established; a form of government much more in keeping with the spirit and genius of the Chinese people than the travesty of a Republic brought about by the Revolution 10 years later.

It was in the Autumn of 1901 that the Court set out on its long trek back to Peking. As the cavalcade advanced at its slow pace of about 20 miles a day it gradually expanded its numbers, in pomp, and in ostentatious display, until it assumed the proportions of a triumphal procession. The approach of the glittering column was notified by fast courier to the mandarins of the larger towns well in advance so that

---

28 [ECP] The Boxer indemnities amounted to £67,500,000, of which the modest British share was £7,500,000.

121

they might have warning to repair and level the roads. Crowds lined the route as the procession passed through the towns and villages, the people kneeling at the road side.

For the passage of the Yellow River a magnificent barge shaped like a colossal dragon, and gorgeously decorated, had been especially built for Her Majesty. The broad river was crossed with imposing pageantry, with a great flutter of flags and beating of drums, with ceremonial oblations to the river-god, and with universal rejoicing.

On passing through Tai-yuan-fu, where she had rested on her outward journey, she again met the Governor, Yu-hsien. He was kneeling outside the city, a little apart from the populace. On seeing him the Old Buddha stopped and addressed him. Leaning from her chair, which was richly decorated and embroidered in Imperial yellow, she expressed her regrets that she was powerless to save him from the punishment to be meted out to him by the foreign devils (decapitation); but added that she had been informed that 'coffins had come down in price', a euphemistic way of suggesting that his best course would be suicide. But the hint was not taken, and in due course, the blood-stained Governor met the fate which he so richly deserved.

On arrival at the capital, the column re-formed, and, passing through the city gates and along the main thoroughfares lined by kneeling troops, reached at length the seclusion of the Imperial Palaces within the Forbidden City. Thus did this artful Jezebel contrive to stage an exultant return, and to 'save her face', when, in all conscience she should have slunk back in ignominy and shame.

The Court was back in Peking, but it was a very much wiser Old Buddha who was now restored to the Dragon Throne. Henceforth she would steer a different course. Not that there was anything like a real change of heart, or that she hated the 'barbarians' any less, but she realised how mistaken had been her anti-foreign regime. Her policy now would be one of appeasement. It would be easy to throw dust into the foreigners' eyes. They were forever talking about China's need for 'reform'. She would make a show of introducing some of those very measures which she herself had so ruthlessly crushed. In adopting this conciliatory attitude Her Majesty was very successful.

Tsu-Hsi was a good actress, and, in a social capacity she could be quite charming. She even proceeded to the unparalleled precedent of inviting the Legation and other foreign ladies to the Palace, there to impress them by her ostentatious display and her gracious condescension. This, no doubt, was all very exciting; but when we remember that it was this same guilty and unrepentant woman who had been responsible for the murder of many of their fellow countrymen and women, and who had indeed attempted to exterminate every one of us, it is regrettable that our women in Peking should have seen fit to accept these invitations. But accept they did, and were of course thrilled to be admitted into the Forbidden City, there to be received by Her Majesty herself. Her outward demeanour was friendly, courteous, and informal. Having been duly impressed by the glamour of an Oriental Court, the guests were escorted by her ladies-in-waiting about the Palace grounds, and on the lakes, and were enchanted by the vistas of island pavilions, marble bridges, flowery grottos, and lotus ponds – while across the water floated the dulcet tones of the temple bells. The Old Buddha certainly knew how to mesmerise the foreigner. A little later an American lady was invited to stay at the Palace to paint Her Majesty's portrait. This she did, and the picture is now the property of the American Nation.

The next few years slipped quietly by; the Dowager again at the helm of the Ship of State, ruling autocratically, but with more circumspection. She was now more willing to be guided, especially in her foreign policy, by the greater wisdom and experience of her chief Adviser, Jung-Lu. She rose early every morning, and never failed to hold her Audiences with the Grand Councillors. Dispatches were constantly arriving from the Provinces relating to problems of local government. To all these matters she gave her immediate attention.

Having despatched the business of the day Tsu His would spend long hours in the open air. She was fond of her lakes and gardens. She possessed considerable artistic talent, and derived enjoyment and relaxation from painting in watercolour on silk: also from her Court theatricals, in which she would occasionally take a part herself.

But as the years passed she grew sad and lonely. Li-Hung-chang[29] died in 1901, and Jung-Lu in 1903. They had been pillars of strength and she missed their wide experience and ripe judgement. From now on she felt more acutely the weight of her responsibility, and her health began to fail.

In 1908 her strength gave way more seriously, and she knew that her end was near. The Emperor, too, fell ill. Remembering his past history one is entitled to doubt whether this could have been mere coincidence. It is practically certain that the Old Buddha took measures to ensure that, after her demise, the Imperial prisoner would not be free to ascend the Throne, or to triumph over her long-awaited departure. He died in November of the same year, and she followed him, at the age of 73, very soon afterwards.

When asked, as the end drew near, for a last message to her people, she is reported to have said, 'Never again allow a woman to hold the supreme power in the State'. Did she realise that her foolish credulity with regard to the magic powers of the Boxers (contrary to the advice and, in such matters, more masculine judgement of Jung-Lu) had, at one time, brought the Empire to the verge of ruin? Or was it jealousy lest any other woman should ever again rise to that height of power and glory in the Dynastic Line to which she had attained?

The funeral rites and solemnities consequent upon the decease of the Empress-Dowager Tsu-Hsi, were upon a most imposing scale. The Imperial Tombs are situated in a noble arena amidst the Eastern Hills, 90 miles from the capital, and here, for the last few years, under Her Majesty's direct supervision, intensive work had been proceeding on the construction of a magnificent mausoleum for the reception of her mortal remains. According to available records the cost of this work was in the neighbourhood of 8,000,000 taels, roughly £1,000,000.

The conveyance of the body to its remote resting place was made the occasion for the parade of the most solemn pageantry. The Catafalque was borne aloft by 120 bearers robed in red. These were preceded by the Princes, the Grand Councillors, and the High Officers of State in

---

29  Li Hung-chang (Li Hongzhang, 1823–1901), modernising statesman and diplomat, supporter of railway construction, telegraphs and a modern naval fleet.

their full regalia. Behind came the Household Cavalry, followed by the Llamist priests draped in yellow.

[one page missing from typescript here]

Being strong-willed she would tolerate no authority but her own, came to her own decisions, and was swift to take action. She has been credited with great wisdom in State-craft; but the wisdom was that of Jung-lu, with whose opinions she generally concurred. Her one great mistake was over the Boxers, when she thrust aside his saner counsels and brought disaster upon the whole country.

There can be no doubt as to the Old Buddha's extraordinary vitality and high courage. Determined to rule without a rival she swept from her path any whom she regarded as potentially dangerous. She would blaze up in fierce anger at any suggestion of opposition. One of her Councillors has recorded that when thwarted her paroxysms of rage were awful to witness. She followed the tradition of her Court, where jealousies, passions, and intrigues were ever rife, and where it was taken for granted that the Monarch's dominant status could be upheld only by acts of vengeance and oppression. The best we can say for her is that she was the product of her environment.

The Old Buddha was avaricious to a degree, and her greed of gain was apparently insatiable. She was possessed of enormous wealth. Her Privy Purse (derived from percentages levied on trade, the harvests and so on, and remitted to Peking by the Provincial Authorities) averaged £5,000,000 per annum. Even while in exile in Hsi-an the value of the 'tribute' exacted from the provinces ran into millions of pounds, and that at a time when the people were suffering great poverty and hardship. Her hoarded fortune, stuffed into the Palace vaults, and consisting of gold Buddhas and pagodas, silks, jade, jewels, objets d'art etc. was computed to be worth £20,000,000.

The new Summer Palace and grounds, in which Her Majesty took such delight, was only made possible by appropriation of funds which had been expressly assigned for the use of the Navy. Although she knew this perfectly well, in her edict issued on entering into possession of the Palace she falsely declared that 'the cost of construction had all been met out of surplus funds accumulated as a result of rigid economies in the past'.

In this same Edict, as in many others, is much nauseating hypocrisy regarding her constant concern for, and strenuous service on behalf of, her people.

Another trait in Tsu-Hsi's character was her inordinate vanity. She loved to be attired in her resplendent, richly embroidered robes. Priceless gems adorned her person. Three and a half thousand magnificent pearls specially selected for their beauty and strung together, composed just one of her lovely capes. She cherished also the most extravagant ideas regarding her origin, believing herself to be the living incarnation of Kwan-yin, the Buddhist Goddess of Mercy, and did not hesitate to speak of herself as 'the most wonderful woman that ever lived'. In this she was heartily supported by her obsequious Court.

But there was a more pleasing side to the Old Buddha. The foreigners who came in contact with her after her return to Peking speak of her courtesy, her fascinating manners, and her charm. Being so good an actress no doubt she could readily assume these qualities in their presence. Her own subjects, Manchus and Chinese alike – especially in the northern provinces – were very proud of her strong person-ality; and her anti-foreign sentiments only enhanced her reputation. Her popular name, 'The Old Buddha', had nothing of disparagement in it. It was the name by which she liked best to be called, and it was used freely and even affectionately by the people. Her life was largely shrouded in mystery. Very little leaked out from the 'Great Within', and consequently we lack the more intimate knowledge that would enable us more accurately to understand the depths of so complex a character. But it was difficult to enthuse over her 'charm' and 'fascination' when one remembers her crimes, her cruel murders, and her vindictive hatred of foreigners.

We have to remember, of course, that the Empress-Dowager was a pagan Monarch, guided by ancient traditions and barbarous prece-dents, and it would be manifestly unfair to judge her by Christian standards. But pagan peoples are not devoid of Conscience, or incapable of distinguishing between Right and Wrong. Moreover Tsu-Hsi was thoroughly familiar with her own Classics, inculcating hospitality and courteous treatment of the stranger. Confucius taught that 'All under heaven are one family' and the Old Buddha herself, in rebuking her officials, was fond of quoting passages from the ancient books, and lecturing them on correct conduct!

Tsu Hsi was the last of the reigning Sovereigns of China.[30] With her passing passed also the Manchu Dynasty which had lasted for 300 years. Soon after her death in 1908 the country was again in the throes of a Convulsion. As a result the Old Order, with its autocratic medieval government, crumbled away, and under the pressure of Republican ideas, gave place to the New. But of the Revolution which brought this about I will speak in a later chapter.

---

30 [ECP] If we except the Child Emperor, Hsuan Tung [Xuantong] (Pu-yi) whose abdication took place in 1912, following the Revolution. By agreement with the Republicans he was allowed to retain the Imperial Title, though bereft of all authority in the State. He held a retired Court in the Great Within until 1924, when he was forced, in quite a brutal manner, to resign his Title, to vacate the Forbidden City, and to retire into private life as an ordinary citizen.

# Chapter XIII

# KULING

After this long digression – in order to give some idea of the history of the Empress-Dowager subsequent to her flight from the capital – I will return to a record of my own personal experiences.

It will be remembered that with the arrival of the Expeditionary Force in Peking the end had come with dramatic suddenness; the Boxer Rising collapsing like a pricked balloon. The wave of destruction which had threatened every foreigner in the country abruptly subsided. The relief to us all in Hankow was intense. Many who had borne up bravely for so long broke down from nervous exhaustion. We were all played out also by the moist heat, which rose at times to 105°F.

As soon as I could make arrangements for the care of such patients as were still on my hands, in company with two or three others, I left Hankow for the mountains of Kuling,[31] in the province of Kiang-hsi [Jiangxi]. We disembarked at the river-port of Kiu Kiang [Jiujiang], nearly 200 miles down stream. It is at this place that some of the finest native porcelain is manufactured; the choicest pieces, decorated with the Imperial five-clawed dragon, being forwarded to the Court at Peking. We looked into one or two work-shops, but had too little time to see how such lovely things were made.

We spent the night at the 'Rest House', a place in Kiu Kiang reserved for the use of foreigners on their way to the mountains. The night was

---

31 [FW] Kuling [Guling] was a mountain resort for foreigners on Lushan, founded by an ex-missionary and ex-chemical salesman, Edward Selby Little. Its name, which had no topographical origin, was meant to suggest the 'cool' refreshing mountain setting.

disturbed by the barking of many dogs, but I was able to snatch a little sleep towards morning.

This proved but a brief respite. We were awakened very early by loud hammering at the door. True to their undertaking on the previous evening the chair and baggage coolies had arrived, bringing with them the open palanquins and carrying poles. They set to work at once on the various pieces of baggage, sorting them out according to weight for equal distribution. By the time we had had a hasty breakfast the loads had been satisfactorily adjusted, and we were off.

The first 10 or 12 miles lay over the flat country bordering the river. It was very hot and steamy as we wound our way in and out between the rice fields. The rice, standing in several inches of water, was well grown and of a lovely green. Innumerable frogs croaked in its cool shade, and here and there were herons, strikingly in harmony with their environment, and looking thoroughly contented in such ideal feeding grounds. Now and again we passed through tiny villages, where our chairs would be unceremoniously dumped down among the pigs and chickens. This gave us an opportunity to stretch our legs, while our sweating coolies imbibed copious draughts of tea. By mid-day we reached the Rest House in the foot-hills, a picturesque wooden building ensconced in a bamboo grove.

After lunch and a good rest we commenced the ascent of the steep mountain side. Roughly laid stone steps, 3 or 4 feet wide, formed a good track all the way up. The bearers were very sure-footed, but from time to time, owing to the steepness, I preferred to climb on foot. It was hard going, but there was ample compensation in the wild scenery, deep glens, turbulent streams, and water-falls. Clumps of bamboo, 30 to 40 feet in height, clothed many of the slopes, and in among the tall grasses were magnificent specimens of trumpet and tiger-lilies.

We reached the bungalow which had been placed at our disposal in the cool of the evening. Standing there on the rugged heights we could catch glimpses of the narrow mountain path by which we had ascended; and beyond the green plain, so far below us, the broad Yang-tse-Kiang was plainly visible.

But what a contrast from the morning! The stifling heat had gone. Now, in the cool invigorating air, renewed life came with every breath. With bodily revival came up-lift of spirits. Depression and weariness dropped from us like a heavy cloak and were replaced by an exuberance and cheerfulness. That night, for the first time for months, we slept under blankets, and without mosquito nets.

The bungalows in Kuling are disposed irregularly up the mountain slopes. There is a native village in 'The Gap', an opening in the mountains leading directly into the main Settlement. Wherever there is a colony of foreigners there is sure to be a 'China-Town' in close proximity. A brisk trade is carried on by the Chinese in supplying the needs of the community. Fresh fruits and vegetables were daily brought up from the plains, and even herds of cattle were introduced into neighbouring valleys to furnish a milk supply. Some of the bungalows were fortunate in having natural springs on their plots, but the main water supply was derived from a central stream. At the far end the stream widened into a broad, deep pool, and then began its precipitous descent through gaps and gorges to the plain 4,000 feet below. This pool, in its wild setting, was a favourite spot for picnic and bathing parties. Here one could get a good high dive from surrounding rocks, and a refreshing swim.

We spent our days in the open air and rapidly regained strength. Long tramps on the mountain heights, and excursions to the many beauty spots – the 'Dragon Pool', the 'Incense Mills', the 'Waterfall', the 'caves', the 'Emerald Pool', the 'Lion's Leap'– completely filled our days, until, at the end of a month's holiday, the time came to return and go our several ways.

When I reached Hankow again and was preparing for my journey back to Hunan, I noticed that there was a very different spirit among the people. This was, of course, due to the fact that the country had 'lost face', and it could not be denied that the foreigner had scored. We were no longer the target for insult and abuse, and practically all danger of physical violence had vanished. One felt it safe to mix with the populace, and to pass down their crowded streets. The threatening demeanour had gone, and even the cry 'Ya, foreign devil!' had died away.

*Two landmarks visited to this day by all who climb Mount Lu: Mervyn Peake must have known both the same pillar rising a thousand metres or more above the valley floor, and the horizontal pine that reappears in Gormenghast, leaning ' 'fantastically into space'.*

Every steamer which now came ploughing up the Yang-tse brought back some of those who had had to flee the country and find refuge in Japan. We all had much to talk about; and there was much speculation as to what the peace terms would be. What was to become of the Old Buddha? Would the Western Powers demand her abdication? Would the Emperor be restored to the throne? What punishment awaited the Boxer leaders, and such malignant ruffians as Yu-hsien? The negotiations proceeding in Peking proved to be very tardy, and it was not until many months afterwards that we learnt the details concerning the demands made by the Powers in the Peace Protocol.

# Chapter XIV

# OVERLAND TO CANTON

Those of us who, during the storm, had gathered in the larger centres for greater safety, now began to disperse. I was glad to be on the move again. Once more, leaving Hankow behind, and accompanied by my two faithful retainers, I made the long boat journey back to Heng-chow.

I was relieved to find, on arrival, that all was in order. The gate-keeper was at his post; there had been no attack on the premises; and my possessions were just as I had left them. This immunity from mob-violence must be attributed to the attitude of the Tao-t'ai, who taking his cue from the Viceroy at Wuchang, had been anxious to maintain order. He paid a complimentary call soon after my return, expressing his deep satisfaction that the troubles were past, and assuring me that the attitude of 'the stupid people' towards 'the honourable gentlefolk' from the Western lands had completely changed. There would be no more trouble, and I could live in peace. He understood that I wished to have the military guard removed, and he would see that this was done. He professed to be keenly interested in my plan for providing the city with a hospital. Might he be permitted, though all unworthy, to make his mean contribution towards the realisation of the scheme.

It was soon evident that the Tao-t'ai was right. I could now go down the street without arousing resentment, and without a crowd following. The prospect for opening up medical work had vastly improved, and I made plans to this end as early as possible.

I decided, in the first place, to start only with out-patients, hoping by this means gradually to break down prejudice. In the course of time, perhaps, patients would lose their fears, and might be induced to come into my small ward as in-patients. Accordingly I settled on the date of the opening day, and this was well advertised in the city.

As zero hour approached I was much occupied in speculating as to results. As a matter of fact only a few men and boys ventured to present themselves; and they came in a bunch as if for mutual protection. All were suffering from the same complaint, the skin affection known as scabies. These were all supplied with sulphur ointment, and carefully instructed as to how it was to be used; that it was not to be swallowed but to be rubbed into the affected parts after cleansing with hot water.

On the following days more and more patients gathered in the waiting-room, but always with the same complaint, scabies! Deriving benefit from the treatment they naturally informed their friends. The numbers applying for relief grew at an amazing rate. The stream became a flood. Literally hundreds applied for the magic medicine. All sorts of receptacles were brought to receive the precious ointment, the most popular being sections of bamboo sawn off near the joints.

Such a commencement to my out-patient work had come as a rather amusing surprise. But I soon found it decidedly monotonous. I had pictured the assembly of many interesting cases and had never anticipated being inundated by throngs of coolies afflicted by such a commonplace skin condition as scabies. Fortunately by using lard (which could be bought on the street) as a base, and with a good barrel of sulphur powder, we were able to keep up an ample supply. As it was merely a matter of dealing out the ointment it was not long before this duty was relegated to the gate-keeper. Yet I think that scabies and sulphur ointment played their part in winning good-will, and in helping to overcome fear and suspicion.

But the weeks and the months slipped by and we seemed to make no further progress. Though outwardly there had been great improvement in the behaviour of the people there was still deep-rooted distrust of the foreign doctor. All sorts of absurd and mendacious tales were in circulation. To consult him the patient might be bewitched and ran the risk of losing his reason. And though the sufferer himself might be willing, it was next to impossible to overcome the opposition of those at home.

At times the situation seemed quite hopeless, but I had no alternative but to hold on and play a waiting game.

★ ★ ★

It was during this passive period (1903) that I again left Heng-chow; this time for the purpose of joining my fiancée at Canton [Guangzhou]. To reach this city by the shortest route it was necessary to proceed overland, travelling due south. I had notified the Tao-t'ai of my intention to make this journey, and he, fearing I might meet with trouble on the way – for it was wild country and unfrequented by foreigners – was anxious that I should not go without an escort. If anything were to happen to me while travelling in his province he would have been involved in serious trouble. It was strange to contemplate how completely the official attitude had changed. The strictest orders from Peking were now reaching the provincial mandarins to protect the foreigners within their areas of jurisdiction. I had, of course, to comply with the Tao-t'ai's wishes, and on the morning of my departure the escort duly arrived at my front gate.

We moved off in the early morning, four braves marched ahead; I came next, riding my pony, with Chow-ling on foot behind. Then six more warriors, and lastly two mounted officers. The baggage coolies trundled along in the rear, with a couple of soldiers behind them. This was a necessary precaution to keep the coolies from lagging, and to guard against their making off with the food and bedding in some wayside village. Thus, in single file, we wound our way through the deserted streets, and out into the open country, following the narrow tracks behind the rice fields. A halt was called for an alfresco breakfast about 11 a.m. then on again to complete the stage before nightfall.

I had already experienced the discomfort of native quarters in a town; I was now to have my first taste of an inn in the country. It had been a hard ride, and I was stiff and fatigued from the unaccustomed ordeal of being all day in the saddle, when we reached our shelter for the night. This proved to be little more than a hovel, a draughty wooden shanty, with a damp mud floor. There was no privacy or comfort anywhere; not even a moderately restful chair. It was winter and the night turned very cold: one could only stand and shiver; concentrate on Mark Tapley[32]; and wait for the baggage coolies, who had been left a long way in the rear. There could be no supper and no bed until their arrival. At length the barking of the village dogs proclaimed the fact that they had turned up at last. Chow-ling immediately pounced upon the provision basket, and in a surprisingly short space of time had produced a hot meal for me – tinned sausages fried over a brazier of glowing charcoal, bread, butter, and tea with condensed milk. The last thing was to roll myself up in my wadded quilt and fall asleep.

We were up again at 5 o'clock the next morning and on the road – a mere stony track – once more. Each day was like the last. It was hard going, and we were a silent company.

Soon after sunset on the fourth day we reached a large town. Here my guard had to report to the chief magistrate of the place and get their discharge; returning to Heng-chow the way we had come and taking my horse back with them. A fresh escort of foot-soldiers was provided for me; and also a 4-bearer mountain chair, for the terrain would soon become so hilly and broken as to be unsuitable for riding.

For the first two days we traversed a well-laid stone-paved road, as a road the best I had yet seen in China. It was about six feet wide, strongly and compactly built, but the stone slabs, worn by the foot of man and beast for centuries, had become highly polished and slippery. The road was part of an ancient highway between Canton and Hankow. Before the days of steamers in Chinese waters, trade from the southern provinces passed northwards over this once famous road. The traffic on it in olden times seems, from all accounts, to have been enormous. Droves of pack-mules with their drivers are said to have crowded the trade-route. There were many unused inns and empty warehouses – relics of the departed glory - and the people bemoaned the fact that the good old days had gone. When the foreign steam-ships appeared the bulk of the trade went round the coast to Shanghai, and then up the Yang-tse. A certain amount of traffic still passes over this ancient road, though a mere trickle compared with former times. I passed numbers of wretched mules heavily laden with salt. Many of them suffered

---

32 [FW] A character in Dickens' novel *Martin Chuzzlewit*, always cheerful and positive.

with cataract and were blind. I noticed that succeeding generations of these poor beasts had worn deep hoof-prints into the hard stone, which, I was told, they made careful use of in wet weather when the road was extremely slippery. I met also long lines of coolies carrying tub-like receptacles filled with vegetable oil. Others were loaded up with bundles of fire-crackers, and bales of tobacco leaf.

We were now approaching the high mountain range which forms the boundary between the two provinces of Hunan and Kuang-tung [Guangdong]. Just before reaching the foot-hills the terrain became level, the road straightened out, and then, to my astonishment, grotesque figures reared their heads above the ground to stare at the foreign devil who had dared to intrude upon their age-long solitude. I felt that these pieces of sculpture, hewn out of solid blocks of hard stone, must have lain there for centuries. The pieces had been placed at regular intervals, and faced one another from both sides of the roadway. They represented savage replicas of the brute creation; rampant lions, elephants, wild boars. The carved figures had been executed with great spirit. Many were weather-worn, tilted over at odd angles, and half buried in the ground, giving the impression of great antiquity. What was their significance? What history lay behind this strangely adorned section of the ancient highway? This can only be matter for idle speculation; but I felt it to be a sad pity that work of such high merit should be thus derelict in the wilderness.

After leaving these relics of a by-gone age, our road passed through the foot-hills and then, degenerating to a mere track, began the steep ascent. After a hard climb we found the 'pass', and then came down on the far side of the range. I had now reached a tributary of the great North River.

From now on my way would be by water. My escort, with Chow-ling, turned back at this point; leaving me, now quite alone, in the midst of a motley crowd on the river bank.

Most fortunately a small boat, carrying tobacco and fire-crackers, was about to start down stream immediately, and I had no difficulty in securing a passage on her. I found that only craft built for navigating the rapids were to be had at this place. When we reached the main river I would have to transfer to a larger boat. So almost as soon as the baggage was on board we were off. We were so heavily laden that I had only just sufficient space to make a narrow bed against the cargo at the stern. The roof-matting, which was wide open at both ends, projected over me and afforded covering immediately above.

The boat, as I have said, was especially constructed for shooting the rapids. It was long, narrow, and high at the prow. A very long and strong oar was pivoted both over the bows and over the stern. These were used for steering between the rocks in the swift treacherous water. They were worked by a lateral stroke, the oars acting as levers, which, by taking a good grip of the water, could be used to turn the craft about at will. When bow and stern sculls (each manned by two men) were used simultaneously and in opposite directions, the boat could be swivelled round at a single stroke.

For two days we were shooting down the most awful-looking water-slides it has ever been my lot to encounter. Time and again I thought we must surely be smashed to bits against the rocks. Sometimes we would swish down at a terrific pace, apparently dead upon some projecting rock, and just when one expected the crash to come one sweep of the long oar would throw the bows to one side, and we would glide swiftly and safely by. Several times we scraped over sunken rocks, which made our timbers creak; but instead of being ripped open, the bottom planks being made of a specially pliant wood, yielded and bulged inwards, causing a wooden wave to run visibly along the bottom. On one occasion however, we did spring a rather bad leak, but this was quickly controlled by caulking the seam up with some soft stringy material. The many wrecks scattered along this part of the river, stranded ashore or impaled on the sharp-pointed rocks, were a forcible reminder of what our fate might so easily have been. In case of ship wreck one could not hope to escape ashore alive owing to the tremendous force of the current and the numerous rocks.

The scenery at first was very wild, the forest-clad hills coming right down to the water's edge. The tiger and the wild boar rove the woods. I caught sight of the latter rooting under the trees. As we progressed rapidly down stream the landscape gradually assumed a more gentle aspect, the river widened, the rocks disappeared, and the strength of the current abated. Huts and fishing boats appeared on the banks, and later villages. Then we reached a town at the effluence into the North River. Here I transshipped to a larger boat.

I had difficulty in understanding the skipper, for, being Cantonese, he spoke a very different dialect. One evening he seemed very concerned about something. At last I found he was trying to tell me that there were pirates lurking on the particular reach of the river, and that we had better get inshore and tie up in a cove for the night. I was anxious to get on and not willing to do this. He was much perturbed until I extracted a very large old-fashioned revolver from the depths of the baggage. On seeing this he brightened up instantly and a very broad grin overspread his weather-beaten countenance. He was now perfectly satisfied and eager to push on. Indeed, he appeared all agog for a scrap, and I suspect was much disappointed when, as it transpired, we were not attacked. I did not spoil the fun by telling him that I had no ammunition!

It was obvious, as we travelled further south, that the country became more and more thickly populated. We passed by large towns; and then, at last, late one evening, we glided into the great metropolis of Canton. The journey had occupied 16 strenuous days (during the latter part of which I had suffered from a sharp attack of dysentery) and we had covered approximately 400 miles.

Our wedding took place in Hong Kong on the last day of the year, and very soon afterwards we were on our way northwards by coastal steamer to Shanghai. Then up the Yang-tse again to Hankow, thence, as before, by house-boat to Hunan. We had good weather during this latter part of the journey, and made good time, taking only 17 days. It was a happy return for me. The hazardous pioneering period was over and our prospects for the future were bright and full of encouragement.

# Chapter XV

# THE CASE OF MR SUNG

I reopened the Out-patient Clinic as soon as possible after arriving back in Heng-chow. The response was reassuring. There seemed to be a new and more friendly spirit in the air. It was not long before many were coming with maladies other than scabies. As the numbers afflicted with the latter trouble became less and less their place was taken by an assortment of cases that proved of real interest.

But conversation was not so easy as formerly, when little need be said and diagnosis could be made at a glance. When questions had to be asked one was up against what appeared to be crass stupidity. There is nothing lacking, however in the mentality of the Chinese patient. It is just that you, and everything about you, is so strange to him that he is struck dumb. From your lighter coloured hair and eyes, your whiter skin and unusual features, your queer clothes, down to your curious leather shoes, you are a droll oddity. He appears bewildered and ill at ease. The consulting room and dispensary, the foreign-style furniture and medical equipment, the whole environment, is new to him. Remember also that he has heard many monstrous stories about you. Is it any wonder that he feels scared?

Under these circumstances I found that to get into human touch with my patients was, at first, by no means easy. Patience and tact were essential in order to gain their confidence and make them feel at home.

The other all-important factor making for success, so far as the foreign physician is concerned, is familiarity with the language. It is the language difficulty which constitutes the real barrier. If that can be broken down and we can converse together in colloquial speech, it will be found that it is not the case that 'East is East', and 'West is West, and never the twain shall meet'.

Many of the patients came in from the country, and these were apt to be more diffident than the town dwellers. The rustic from some outlying villages comes into your room more shyly, and perhaps suffering a little from 'stage-fright'. He looks awkwardly about him. Never having seen such a curious object on the floor (the door-mat) he makes a careful detour round it. There is an empty chair next to your desk, and, after some hesitancy, he is persuaded to sit down. A medical friend of mine[33] has given a graphic description of the kind of dialogue that ensues as follows:

'What is your honourable name?'

'Ah!'

'What is your name?'

'Fever every third day; it began —'

'Listen! What is your name?'

'Name Wong. Fever for over two months; my —'

'Where do you live?'

'The Wong-family village; the fever is very bad; he has taken medicine, and he is no better; please give me good medicine. The doctor has a great name.'

'Is it you, or somebody else, who is ill?'

'Both of us. I came for medicine; it is a very long way —'

'If two people want medicine each must be attended separately. How far do you live from the city?'

'I started after my morning rice.'

'Is it over thirty li?' (i.e. about 10 miles)

'Over twenty li.'

'What is your age?'

'I was born in the year of the dragon.'

'Ah! How much older are you than thirty?'

'I'm only twenty-nine.'

At last we have the items we wish to enter in the Register, and from his description express our opinion that he is suffering from malaria.

---

33 [ECP] Dr H. Fowler of Hsiao-Kan [Xiaogan], Hupeh [Hubei] Province.

'Yes, my fever is every third day; his is every day, and he has the itch too, all over him.'

'I have already told you that we only attend one patient at a time; but I will give you some ointment for the other one.'

We begin to write his prescription, and his attention is attracted by the queer foreign pen, and the extraordinary marks it is making. He rises and bends over to inspect it. This is something to talk about when he gets back to his village; he must have a good look! The assistant gives him his prescription, with his hand on the bell impatient to to ring in the next one, but gives him at the same time careful instruction as to taking his medicine.

'Is it wet medicine or dry medicine?'

'It is drinking medicine.'

'Ask the doctor to give me dry medicine. I have no bottle.'

'You can buy one from the gate-keeper. Take your prescription and get your medicine from the medicine room. When it is finished come back again. There are six days' medicine. Do you understand?'

The bell has rung and another patient has come in, but still he sits there till the assistant takes his arm and gently pushes him to the door. With a sigh of relief we apply ourselves to the next case.

In such cases as the above, where an ointment is prescribed for the skin trouble and a quinine for the malaria, it would be necessary to be very explicit as to which is for external and which for internal use; otherwise it is quite possible that the ointment will be swallowed, and the mixture rubbed over the body, three times a day after meals! Quick results are expected. If the first dose does not cure or relieve it is probable that the medicine will be thrown away and that he will not trouble to come again. And even if he does come repeatedly it is quite likely that between his visits he will seek the advice of some local quack.

So I found, in those early days, that the out-patient practice was in many ways very unsatisfactory. And yet, apart from its psychological value, it did yield useful results; and moreover it was only from the out-patients that I could hope to draw my in-patients. I saw many good cases requiring surgical treatment. I hoped that confidence was growing, and so prepared the 6-bed ward in readiness to receive any who might be courageous enough to come in.

But for a very long time the ward remained empty. The people had gathered sufficient courage to attend as out-patients, to be questioned and examined, and to take the foreign medicines; but no one could be found who would remain under the foreign doctor's roof. Over and over again it would be explained to a patient that his condition was curable, but that it would be necessary for him to come into my ward and have an operation.

What did an operation mean? Would not taking some of the honourable doctor's very best medicine have the desired result, without having to recourse to 'cutting the disease' (kwo ping )? And what about pain? Was it true that the doctor possessed some wonderful 'stupefying medicine' (ma yoh) which made the patient sleep so deeply that he could be cut without being wakened, and without pain? Then would follow some explanation of the nature of the required operation, and how complete insensibility could be induced by inhaling the vapour of a clear liquid which looked like water (chloroform).

These conversations never failed to excite the greatest interest: but to be the first to submit himself to the doctor's magic sleeping medicine, and to his knife, required unusual courage. Occasionally one or another, driven by his disability or suffering, would come to the verge of decision, only to be dissuaded by his relations and friends. I felt confident that if but one good surgical case would consent to operation, given good results, others would follow. That was my hope; but though the out-patients continued to increase, and I saw a good many cases, yet for a long and tantalising time no one was found sufficiently daring to take the plunge.

At last the opportunity came in the person of Mr Sung, an intelligent old gentleman over 70 years of age, a scholar, well-known and highly respected in the city. But he was blind. When I arrived in the consulting room that morning there was quite a little stir among my small staff. They were not accustomed to see such distinguished people among the out-patients. It was evident that Mr Sung had plucked up courage, and led by his man-servant through the narrow winding streets, had come to see if the foreign doctor could do anything for him.

After the usual polite formalities, and Mr Sung was seated, he explained to me that his blindness had come on gradually during the last few years, and was now complete. Could anything be done for his eyes? It only required a brief examination to make it quite clear that he was suffering from cataract.

Cataract is a disease of the eye in which the lens is affected. The small crystalline lens situated immediately behind the pupil is, normally, clear and transparent. Its function is to refract the rays of light and to focus them upon the retina behind. In cataract the lens loses its transparency. It gradually becomes more and more opaque until light is completely excluded and the patient becomes blind. Cure of this condition is effected by removal of the cataractous lens by operation, thereby allowing light to reach the retina, and so restoring vision.

I explained to Mr Sung the cause of his trouble, and also that it would be necessary for him to come into my small ward for treatment. His ready assent, so entirely unexpected, quite took my breath away. Here was just the kind of case I had been waiting for. A well-known and influential citizen, who had derived no benefit at the hands of the native practitioner, had come along to see if the foreign doctor could help him. And it was just that dramatic type of case that would appeal to the popular imagination. If indeed an operation was successful in restoring this patient's vision, a sensation of the first magnitude would be created among the people, and the medical work would receive a great forward impetus. To restore sight to the blind was something quite unheard of, and nothing short of the miraculous. On the other hand for the operation to fail would be calamitous. It would, in the popular view prove our enemies and detractors to be right. Not only had the foreign doctor completely failed, but he had taken his knife out and cut into the patient's eyes. Here was positive proof of his diabolical practices. Could anything be more conducive to raising the angry passions of the mob, which might well result in active demonstrations of hostility, if not of actual riots? I had been waiting for such an occasion as this, but now that it presented itself I became acutely aware of the weight of my responsibility. The situation was almost frightening. Yet I had no alternative but to proceed. Risks must be taken, and this wonderful opportunity must not be allowed to slip by for lack of courage on my part. So Mr Sung came in.

It was with some trepidation that, a day or two after his coming, I operated on the right eye. My wife, who was acting as nurse, and my few assistants stood around the head of the table and watched my every movement. A local anaesthetic dropped into the eye abolished sensation. A speculum held the eye-lids widely open. Then in an atmosphere of tense expectancy I introduced the narrow blade which cut open the front of the eye. To my relief my hand was steady in spite of the nervous strain. Through the incision the opaque lens was successfully extracted. I then held up three fingers and asked the patient to count them. He answered correctly – 'Three'. There was wonderment, and a sigh of relief all round. The ordeal was over. All had gone well, and the outlook was full of hope. The eye was now covered and the patient put back to bed. When, some days later, the bandage was removed, it was found that the wound had healed well, and that sight had been restored. The operation on the left eye, undertaken a fortnight afterwards, was equally successful.

Mr Sung could now see, but, owing to the removal of his natural lenses, his vision was blurred and indistinct. He required artificial lenses, i.e. spectacles with convex glasses, to take their place. These I was able to procure for him from Shanghai. With his precious spectacles he was able to see clearly. I remember well his delight when, walking in the courtyard the evening before he left, he looked up into the heavens and saw the stars.

## THE SEQUEL

My first in-patient had been a great success. The story of Mr Sung had spread through the city. Here was a concrete case that the people could see for themselves. The event was regarded as a marvel and created a big sensation, which was immediately reflected in the numbers crowding the out-patient clinic. Mr Sung himself, in his own home, never tired of recounting to his visitors his unheard of experiences. And he did more than talk.

One morning Ah-shin burst somewhat unceremoniously into my sanctum. 'Come Sir, come and see!' he exclaimed. Knowing Ah-shin's excitable disposition I was not inclined to take him too seriously, but on this occasion it was clear that something quite out of the ordinary was taking place. I rose slowly from my table, where I had been wrestling with Chinese ideograms, inwardly blessing Ah-shin for his untimely interruption. 'What is it Ah-shin?' I said. 'The blind people, doctor', he replied. 'Lots of them, they're coming down the road to our gate!'

Although I could hardly believe him, I followed Ah-shin to a point of vantage where I could look down the narrow street. 'There, look!' he said. Sure enough, coming down the congested thoroughfare and mingling with the colourful medley of a Chinese highway, was a long single file of bedraggled and apparently dejected men. They kept orderly formation, following each other closely and yet at equal distances, with heads bowed and shoulders bent. Looking more carefully at this string of obviously blind people I observed that each man had hold of the pigtail of the one immediately in front of him. At the head of the column I at once recognised Mr Sung. The whole story stood revealed in the street scene before me. Mr Sung had been busy. The foreign doctor had restored his sight. He would tell the good news to others. He would gather the blind together and organise a procession to the clinic, and he himself would lead them. The crowd, aware that something unusual was going on, stood aside and stared.

They were now approaching our front gate, so I despatched Ah-shin with instructions to hasten and warn the gate-keeper. The latter was to admit them without delay and close the gates before the crowd had had time to crush in and get out of hand. Ah-shin, thoroughly enjoying himself, hurried off, and I soon had the satisfaction of seeing the gate cautiously opened and the long line passing into the fore-court. The gates were then closed before the gaping crowd had recovered from their rapt attention and had surged through in their wake.

When I reached the consulting room my first case was to interview Mr Sung. He was ushered into my room, and having made a deep bow,

146

was persuaded, after protesting his 'unworthiness', to take a seat. It was evident that Mr Sung was carefully attired for the occasion. His head was freshly shaved, his queue neatly plaited, and he wore a handsome silk gown. Ah-shin now appeared and placed cups of tea before us.

The preliminary ceremonies being concluded I glanced across at Mr Sung and noticed that his face was wreathed in smiles. And a very attractive old face it was, gentle and kindly, with well-marked lines of sagacity and experience. His venerable appearance was enhanced by the silky white beard which flowed in a narrow stream over his breast.

'Mr Sung', I said, 'tell me about all these people that you have brought along today'.

'Honourable Sir', he replied, addressing me in his characteristically courteous and complimentary manner, 'You will remember that when I left this House of Healing, after your consummate skill had restored to me the use of my eyes, I made known to you my resolve to publish abroad the beneficent work which you are doing for the inhabitants of this city. Especially it was my wish to help those afflicted with diseases of the eye and blindness, of whom there are, as your Excellency knows, very many in this place. I have also made it my duty to refute the ridiculous rumours which are current with regard to your honourable self. I have visited homes where I knew there were sufferers and have related to the inmates my wonderful experience. Many of these still hang back, but, on the other hand, there are others who are eager to follow my example. I arranged that these should meet outside the Lung Wang Miao (the Temple of the Dragon King) before mid-day today, and I found, when I arrived there myself, that quite a crowd had collected. I marshalled them in single file, and so led them to the gates of your benevolent Hall of Healing. And now, Sir, you know the rest, for I believe that you witnessed our arrival. I have but one regret. It is that I am the occasion of causing such infinite trouble to your Excellency. For this I humbly crave your forbearance and tender 10,000 apologies.'

'The story which you have unfolded does you very great credit, Mr Sung', I said. 'Please do not apologise for bringing these patients to me here. To relieve such is the very purpose for which the medical work has been started. I will gladly do what I can for them. But you will, of course, understand that some diseases of the eye are much more amenable to treatment than are others. Many I fear will be beyond the reach of either medicine or surgery. There are bound to be some who will be disappointed. But we will look into every case and do our best for each one. I hope that there will be some at least that we can help'. At this point Mr Sung rose, and with another deep obeisance, and further expression of gratitude took his leave.

I now examined each case gathered in the waiting room. One by one, at the stroke of the bell, they were led into my room. Taken as a whole they represented quite an interesting assortment of eye affections. Only a few were likely to derive benefit from operative treatment, others were reluctant to attend as out-patients. But some, with eyes wholly destroyed by small-pox, or incurably blind from other causes, had to be told of their hopeless condition. It was then that painful scenes ensued. Under the impression that they had unwittingly offended me, perhaps by not observing correct etiquette, those unfortunates, in spite of efforts to restrain them, would drop on their knees, and bump their foreheads to the ground in supplication. Explanations were useless. I had cured Mr Sung: this, to them, was proof that I could cure them also. How was one to convince them that refusal to use 'the foreign knife' was not due to unwillingness on the doctor's part but to his genuine inability to help them? For the incurables nothing remained but a return home in bitter disappointment. It was with mixed feelings therefore that I brought the clinic to a close.

Even so, after the case of Mr Sung, the medical work steadily increased. From a narrow trickle, it expanded to a wide and steady stream. At first, as it was supposed that the foreign doctor was competent to deal only with scabies and with eye infections, our clinics were composed almost entirely with such cases. But as time went on the percentage of other pathological conditions showed a marked rise, and long before the clinic opened the waiting room would fill each day with a miscellaneous assortment of ailing humanity.

It was thus that the medical work in the city of Heng-chow was started. As suspicion and ill-will abated, and evil rumours died down, the fame of the 'House of Healing' spread far beyond the boundaries of the prefecture. From distant towns and villages, from scattered hamlets and farms, by boat, by sedan-chair, and wheel-barrow they were brought in. Aged parents would sometimes be carried on the backs of filial sons, and sick babies conveyed in baskets suspended from carrying poles. With our limited accommodation only the selected few could be admitted as in-patients; but the numbers increased so rapidly and the need was so urgent that a new and properly equipped hospital became a necessity.

And in the fullness of time it came.

# Chapter XVI

# THE CLINIC

After Mr Sung had shown the way, the daily clinics were, as I have said, crowded with eye cases and these showed a very wide range.

There was one infective condition, known as trachoma, which I found to be very common. It attacks the under surface of the eye-lids resulting in the growth of painful granulations. The disease can be dealt with and cured if taken in good time; but if neglected, as all our cases were, it leads to inversion of the lids, so that the eyelashes are turned inwards and rub over the surface of the eye. This constant friction leads to inflammation and loss of transparency of the cornea, resulting ultimately in blindness. Numbers of these cases were relieved by a simple operation which corrected the inversion and caused the eye-lashes to stand out again in their natural position.

Many other cases of blindness were due to dead white opacities: situated immediately in front of the pupil – the result of previous ulceration. Here the operation to restore vision is to remove a small portion of the iris above or to one side of the opacity, thus making an artificial pupil, or little window, through which the light could enter.

But the number of patients suffering from other complaints steadily increased and gave a good idea of the diseases commonly met with in South China. They showed that the Chinese have all the ailments that we have in Europe, with their own tropical diseases in addition. Besides the appalling prevalence of eye and skin diseases, I found that digestive disorders were also very common indeed. One got the impression that nearly all adults suffered from dyspepsia. Nor did this surprise me when I saw the gross way in which the people stuff themselves with rice – lifting the full bowl to the mouth and shovelling it in at astonishing speed with their chop-sticks. It seemed to me a marvel that the human stomach could stand such treatment so long and so patiently.

Diseases of the respiratory apparatus were far from uncommon. In the cold season bronchitis was frequently met with. Asthma one saw only occasionally, and I did not see much of pneumonia and pleurisy. But on the other hand tubercular disease of the lungs I found to be exceedingly prevalent. Indeed tuberculosis in all its forms was rampant. In adults, generally the lungs; in children, the neck glands, joints, and bones. I have notes of a small boy of 8 who remained under our care for several months. In his case both ankles, both knees, one wrist, and one elbow were affected.

Rheumatism, sciatica, neuritis, and fibrositis, were common, but among the diseases only rarely encountered were gout, diabetes, and appendicitis. Diseases of the nervous system too, were not often seen, and I got the impression that insanity was relatively infrequent compared with Western peoples.

Then there were the diseases commonly found in the tropics. The chief of these was malaria. Dysentery too, of a very severe type, was very common, and cholera, occurring from time to time in raging epidemics, would sweep through the city and carry off many thousands of victims. Small-pox was always with us, and also typhus, typhoid, and relapsing fever. Occasionally I saw cases of leprosy, kala-azar, beri-beri, and elephantiasis.

Tropical diseases due to the invasion of the human body by a variety of parasites were constantly encountered, and offered an interesting field for research. Of the grosser kinds, one could not long be in medical work in China without being struck by the extraordinary prevalence of worm infections. With the idea of ascertaining the approximate percentage of the population harbouring intestinal parasites I made a microscopic examination of specimens from 150 consecutive and entirely unselected cases. These patients came for various complaints, but not for verminous infection, of which they were unaware. Eggs of one or more species of worms were present in 137 of the 150 cases, and at least 4 different kinds of worms were represented. This gives a result of over 90%, and

I am confident that this is an under-statement, as eggs are scarce in some specimens and can only be found on repeated examination. I very seldom made more than the rapid scrutiny of one microscopic slide. The parasite known as the hook-worm, which was exceedingly common in the agricultural inhabitants of the district, was – and I've no doubt still is – responsible for a great deal of sickness and anaemia. In addition to the four commoner species of worms there was another and deadlier variety (*Schistosomum japonicum*) which I shall have occasion to refer to again later.[34] This latter type came from special endemic foci, and did not occur, like the others, in all grades of the general population.

Analysing 1,000 cases taken seriative from the out-patient register I found that the composition of an average daily clinic, in the early years was roughly as follows:

Diseases of the Eye . . . . . . . . . . . . . . . . . . . . . .22.5%
    " " "        Skin . . . . . . . . . . . . . . . . . . . . . 19%
    " " "        Digestive System . . . . . . . . . . . .7.5%
    " " "        Heart and Lungs . . . . . . . . . . . . 5%
    " " "        Bones and Joints . . . . . . . . . . . . 6%
Venereal Diseases . . . . . . . . . . . . . . . . . . . . . . . 6%
Tropical  " "     . . . . . . . . . . . . . . . . . . . . . . . 14%
Surgical and Miscellaneous . . . . . . . . . . . . . . . . 20%
                                           100%

Surgical cases were very numerous. Tumours and malignant growths were often in such an aggravated form as to be positively grotesque. These required major operative treatment for their removal. So the idea became prevalent that the foreign doctor cured all his patients by 'cutting the disease'. Cases not of a surgical nature at all begged to be 'cut': under the impression that a cure must speedily result if only the doctor would consent to use the knife, whereas, formerly, the mere mention of an operation would scare them away, later on they were frequently disappointed when told that 'cutting' was not indicated in their case.

---

34 [FW] See Chapter XVIII. The eradication of schistosomiasis was one of Mao Zedong's great campaigns of the 1950s, and apparently had some success although the problem still remains.

Nevertheless, working with young and inexperienced assistants, major operative work was hazardous. There was still a large prejudiced section of the people who would have been only too pleased to make things uncomfortable for the foreign devil. The death of a patient under chloroform would have given our enemies a grand pretext for stirring up trouble, and the danger of mob violence was not a remote one.

I recall the case of a young man suffering from a surgical condition who came from a city about 100 miles to our south-east. He explained that his father had strenuously opposed the idea of his consulting the foreign doctor and had forbidden him to do so, but he had managed to get away from home on the pretext of business. However, the old man must have had his suspicions, for on the evening before the operation the patient's elder brother arrived in hot haste to see if the run-away was with us, and if so to bring him away at once. This created an embarrassing situation on the eve of the operation, disobedience to parents being so seriously regarded in China. The patient, however, begged me not to hesitate, and I felt justified in proceeding with the case. All went well and the result was entirely satisfactory. We heard afterwards that no one was more pleased than the old father himself when he had received his son back safe and sound and cured of his trouble.

The first death, following immediately on an operation, did not occur for 8 years after the commencement of the medical work. This happened in the case of a boy on whom I operated for tubercular disease of the knee-joint. The trouble was of long standing, and the disease far advanced. He begged constantly for an operation, but as he was so weak I was reluctant to risk it. But at the end of a month, when his general condition had improved, the task was at length undertaken. I found the joint extensively invaded necessitating the removal of large portions of bone. While still on the table the heart became so weak that the proceedings had to be hastened and terminated as quickly as possible. But the patient never rallied from the shock and died on the evening of the second day. Fortunately no trouble ensued on this our first fatal case. The boy's circumstances were well understood, and the confidence of the people remained unshaken.

# Chapter XVII

# EMERGENCY CALLS

It was after the work had got well started, and the people had become more friendly, that I began to receive calls to attend patients in their own homes. These were, invariably, very serious cases. Frequently I was called in as a last resort, and only after the native practitioners had been in attendance and had 'queered the pitch'. The majority of these urgent calls were either to women in complicated labour, or to suicides.

In a large city like Heng-chow, with a populace of approximately 200,000, difficult labour was of frequent occurrence. The Chinese doctor possessed no obstetrical knowledge whatever. When things went wrong, and there was no possibility of delivery without skilled intervention, the poor woman in her extremity had no one to whom she could turn except the native midwife. Over the methods and habits of the latter it would be charitable to draw a veil. Completely ignorant, filthy, and full of superstitions, 'Sairey Gamp' was an angel in comparison. Not that I wish to heap reproaches upon her. She had no opportunity of knowing any better than her predecessors and was but the product of her environment.

Child-birth was regarded with dread, and the whole process of labour was riddled, in the public mind, by a farrage of foolish and paralysing superstitions. All gave the confined woman as wide a berth as possible; with the exception of the popo – the old midwife – who hovered around the bed muttering charms and hocus-pocus in a hoarse whisper to ward off the evil spirits. Incense must be burned to the gods, and the devils driven away with fire-crackers. Afterwards, when all is over, and in order to avert family disaster, superstitious rites and irksome rules must be observed until the moon has gone full cycle.

It is appalling to think of the suffering endured by thousands of the women of China who die daily, unrelieved by competent assistance; and it is salutary that we should sometimes pause to count our own blessings, not the least of which has been the growth in obstetric knowledge, and the scientific and cleanly treatment of our maternity cases.

With regard to my own experiences, owing to the prejudice against employing a male doctor – and he a foreigner – it was only at the last gasp, when the woman had remained undelivered for days (perhaps even for a week), and was already in extremis, and the child in all probability more than dead, that I was called in. No wonder my heart sank when the call came to 'tsieh-seng' (receive life); and it sank still lower when, on entering the mud hut among the rice fields or the dark city tenement, I was confronted by dirt and squalor and complete unreadiness.

Frequently the wretched apartment was of such flimsy construction that neighbours, knowing the foreign doctor had arrived on the scene, had plenty of opportunity for peering through the crevices to see what was going on. On one occasion, in a hut in the country, there being a space between the wall and the eaves of the roof, some boys outside had climbed up, and, clinging on with their hands, were peering over the top. I got rid of them by rapping their knuckles sharply with my riding whip.

On arrival at the house you find a woman lying on a rickety bed which takes up nearly all the available space. A grunting pig reclines on the mud floor in one corner, and chickens run in and out. Owing to the superstitious belief that stains on one's clothing from such a case would bring bad luck, it is with difficulty that anyone can be found to give you any assistance. All the inmates of the house appear to be petrified and keep aloof. You ask for hot water. Hot water! That's the last thing they would have thought of; but they will get some. About half-a-pint of water, of a very dubious quality is put to boil in a small receptacle on the charcoal brazier. Eventually you get more and more water going. You get the animals driven out, and the place tidied up a bit. At last you are able to turn your attention to the patient.

A general anaesthetic was always necessary in these cases, unless indeed, that it was found that the patient was so far gone that it was useless to attempt anything. My wife frequently helped me as anaesthetist; but sometimes I had to persuade one of the female relatives, or a neighbour, to hold the mask over the patient's face and to keep dropping the liquid on to it as I told her. It was under such circumstances that prolonged and difficult obstetric operations, such as craniotomy, had to be performed. The marvel is that so many of these women recovered. Many a time I have felt quite sure that had the patient been a European she could not have survived. Years later, when we had the facilities, such cases would be removed to the women's hospital. There major operations, such as Caesarean section, could be undertaken under clean conditions, and the lives of both mother and child saved.

The other class of emergency cases to which I had urgent calls were the suicides. Suicide is very common in China. The usual motive appeared to be revenge. There had perhaps been a big quarrel. Then one of the aggrieved parties, unable to obtain satisfaction in any other way, would take his own life, preferably upon his enemy's door-step. His spirit would then be free to haunt, torment, and bring misfortune upon his adversary. The latter would have to admit that the last point had been scored heavily against him.

There were other motives, of course. Accustomed to hardship – for the most part most patiently borne – life, for the majority, was cheap, and held little of real worth. It did not take much to tip the scale in the wrong direction, and suicide would sometimes be resorted to for reasons which would appear to us quite trivial. I remember the case of a beggar, who, with two silver dollars (the equivalent of about 4/-) on his person, fell asleep in the sunshine by the road-side. On waking, and finding that he had been robbed, his first concern was to do away with himself.

The means on which most relied for the purpose of self destruction was by taking poison, and the two chief agents employed were opium and nitric acid. At first it was nearly always opium, and these were exhausting and troublesome cases. Very often the patient was already in a drowsy condition, and had to be constantly aroused and kept from lapsing into a stupor while antidotes were being administered. In cases which were already comatose artificial respiration had to be employed, sometimes for quite long periods. Some such cases were pulled back to life, but for many others all treatment was unavailing.

In the course of time opium became more difficult to obtain, and then recourse was had to nitric acid. This was a cheap, but very strong, commercial acid used for printing patterns on cotton fabric, and it could very readily be bought on the street. The effects of swallowing this strong acid are much more terrible than those which follow the taking of suicidal doses of opium. In the latter drowsiness supervenes, which deepens into a profound coma from which the patient never awakes. He either dies soon, or the means used to save him result in his complete recovery. But in the case of a powerful caustic like nitric acid, the mouth, throat, and stomach sustain terrible damage; the mucous membrane of these parts is corroded, and there follows extensive destruction of tissue, and ulceration. The pain is intense. But, worst of all, in the attempted healing of the ulcerated parts, scar tissue is formed, which contracts more and more, ultimately causing complete obstruction of the gullet. Soon the patient is unable to swallow food; then as the constriction becomes tighter, even semi-solid food will not pass; and lastly it is with the greatest difficulty that he can swallow any liquid at all. The outcome is a slow death from starvation.

There were, of course, other emergencies of a miscellaneous character, but in the main they fell into one or other of these two groups, desperate maternity cases or suicides. These visits into the homes of the people sufficed to raise a corner of the curtain and afforded glimpses of much misery and despair behind the scenes. It is comforting to think of the gradually increasing amelioration of these sorrows which growing contact with the West is bringing to the long-suffering people of China.

# Chapter XVIII

# RESEARCH

I have mentioned the prevalence in southern China of a variety of tropical diseases due to the invasion of the human body by diverse animal parasites. These diseases, not met with at home, were of fascinating interest, and opened up a most alluring prospect for exploration and research. A post-graduate course of study at the London School of Tropical Medicine had inspired me with great keenness for investigation into the parasitology of warm climates. Now that the confidence of the people had to a large extent been gained, and the medical work could carry on quietly and unopposed, I felt that I could turn my attention to some of the puzzling cases which not infrequently presented themselves at the daily clinic. To follow up some of these tropical conditions appealed to me in the nature of an exciting adventure.

There was one class of case that particularly interested me. These patients all made much the same complaint. They spoke of weakness, indigestion, bouts of fever, and dysenteric symptoms. They were listless, enfeebled, emaciated, and quite unfit for any physical or mental effort. Sleep was often disturbed by fever and restlessness. It was obvious that these patients suffered acutely, and that they were seriously ill. The disease was a deadly one. It ran its relentless course unchecked, the patient ultimately dying in a state of extreme exhaustion.

On examination I found that though the bodies of these patients were so emaciated, the abdomen was often enormously distended with dropsical fluid.[35] There was tenderness and enlargement of both liver and spleen, and great engorgement of the veins below the waist. In

---

35 [ECP] In one case the fluid withdrawn from the abdominal cavity measured 30 pints.

short, the signs suggested that there must be some obstruction to the return flow of blood through the liver. Other causes for this obstruction having been eliminated, might it not be due to an invasion of the liver by some noxious worm; and might not the presence of such a parasite be revealed by the discovery of its egg?

I had seen these strange cases as early as 1900, but at that time I had not been in a position to deal with them. Nor did I possess laboratory facilities. But when I could do so I admitted a case into my ward for investigation. Having now my own small laboratory I took the first opportunity to make a microscopical examination of the patient's dejecta. To my astonishment I was instantly rewarded, for there in the prepared film under my microscope were ova of a species of worm I had never before encountered. They were transparent, beautifully oval eggs, showing clearly a double outline. Presently I discovered that the double contour was due to the very thin shell on the outside, and within this, also quite clearly defined, the outline of the contained embryo, which occupied practically the whole length of the egg. But using a more powerful lens I saw that the embryo was covered with fine hair-like lashes, known as cilia. There was a distinct nipple-like protrusion, or papilla, at what was evidently the head end of the embryo, and this papilla showed lively twisting wriggling movements. Within the embryonic proto-plasm one could detect subtle molecular changes constantly going on. I had mounted the specimen on a glass slide, mixed with a drop of plain water, over which was a 'cover-slip', so that the material was pressed into a thin film between the two glass surfaces.

At this point I was called away; but returning to the specimen an hour later, and finding that the water was drying up from under the cover-glass, I added another drop. Almost immediately after supplying the drop of fresh water the eggs began to hatch out. The shells simply ruptured, the embryos escaped, and by movement of their cilia swam gracefully about the microscopic field. I will admit that I was excited. So far as I knew I was the first to discover the hidden cause of a most devastating disease. I was keen to follow the matter up; in particular, to trace the life-history of this new parasite; and to discover, if I could, how it effected its entry into the human body.

Meanwhile I published articles in the medical journals, and corresponded with Specialists in tropical diseases. My old teacher, Sir Patrick Manson, to whom I sent specimens, wrote saying though it was difficult to be positive, in his opinion the ova were those of the new blood-worm *Schistosomum japonicum*. This was a little disappointing, for if Sir Patrick was right then I was *not* the first to report both the disease and its cause. In course of time I was able to confirm the correctness of Manson's diagnosis. The name suggested that the disease was known in Japan. I learnt that in 1904, i.e. three years previously to my own independent discovery, Professor Katsurada of Tokyo University had found the ova in several cases under his care. He carried his investigations further afield, and visiting the endemic area he found the same eggs in two cats, and the worm itself in large numbers in the veins of the bowel and liver. The same symptoms were manifest in Katsurada's cats as in his patients. He described the body of the adult worm as being on average 10–15 millimetres in length (nearly half an inch). The parasite, and the fatal disease caused by it, were new to science, but priority of discovery must go to Katsurada.

Subsequently, when through the medical periodicals attention had been drawn to the subject, news began to come in from doctors in different parts of China (chiefly from endemic foci in the Yang-tse valley) reporting the presence of the trouble in their localities. Indeed, in a comparatively short time it came to be recognised that the parasite had a wide, though patchy, distribution, and that the male population of whole villages was affected. Besides China and Japan it was later reported also from the Philippines.

How does the worm gain entrance into its human host? In a person whose internal organs are infested by the parasite the eggs pass out from the body in prodigious numbers. But these eggs will perish unless they reach water. This can readily be proved in the laboratory. Having reached water of summer temperature and hatched out, the only way in which the swarms of free-swimming embryos can effect an entrance into man is through the skin. If taken into the stomach in drinking-water the acidity of the gastric juice would prove fatal to them.

The knowledge that the embryos could only live in water, and the

160

practical certainty that they could only gain an entrance through the skin,[36] combined with the fact that the women were exempt, suggested that the disease was occupational in origin. And that is exactly what we found. The patients were invariably of the male sex; fishermen and boatmen, but mainly coolies from the inundated rice-fields; men who were constantly in and out of the water: frequently standing in the liquid for hours together, and thus exposing large areas of skin surface to infection. This made it clear why the female sex escaped the disease. They were occupied in the home, and did not work in the water like the men and boys. Moreover their bound feet and legs were always well covered, and never bare; thus they were protected even if by occasional chance they came into contact with infected water. I understand that in Japan, where there is no foot-binding, the women frequently suffer, for they are accustomed to help the men, standing bare-legged for more or less lengthened periods in the flooded paddy-fields.

Having hatched out, and undergone certain developmental changes in a species of water-snail, the microscopic creatures, on regaining the water, penetrate the skin, and carried first by the lymph and then by the blood stream, finally reach the veins of those organs for which they have a special predilection, notably the liver and the bowels. Here the parasite makes its home, and begins to grow steadily. As the myriad worms attain adult size and pair, numberless eggs are produced.

The small veins of the liver become blocked, thus offering serious impediment to the passage of blood upwards from the lower half of the body. It is this backward pressure which determines the excessive accumulation of fluid in the abdominal cavity. The dysenteric symptoms are due to the presence of the worm in the intestinal veins causing patches of the mucous membrane to break down and ulcerate, resulting in the discharge of mucus, blood, and countless ova.

The low-lying, steamy plains and muddy levels of the Yang-tse valley form the breeding grounds par excellence for the activities of this

---

36 [ECP] The lethal effect of hydrochloric acid on the embryo can really be demonstrated in the laboratory. A 1% solution of the acid will kill them immediately. Moreover, if it were possible for infection to take place through the mouth the woman also would frequently contract the disease. I never saw a case in a woman.

parasite. The conditions of high temperature and stagnant water are here ideally fulfilled. These also are the requirements for the successful cultivation of the rice crops during the hot summer months when the coolies are busy in the paddy-fields. Of course the water must first be contaminated. But this contamination is going on all the time. The workers themselves are constantly increasing the degree of defilement by their promiscuous and insanitary habits. Unknown to the simple coolie the contact of such polluted water with his bare legs is 'asking for trouble'. Taking advantage of their microscopic dimensions the embryos insinuate themselves through the skin – probably along the hair follicles – and thus gain an entrance into their unsuspecting host.

As might be expected no race is immune. Foreigners who go shooting, and wade bare-legged in the water after duck and snipe, have, not infrequently, been infected. But such can be warned of the danger and so avoid it. It is otherwise with the native population. They must cultivate their rice fields just as their fore-fathers have done for countless generations. To explain the nature of the malady, and to persuade whole populations to wear protective leggings, would be an altogether impossible task; and in any case such advice would not be heeded. Thus treatment of these patients was of necessity individual and symptomatic; at the same time warning him of the source of his trouble, and, to the best of one's ability, putting him on his guard against fresh incursions by such unwelcome guests.

The invasion of man by this noisome parasite was to me a subject of absorbing interest, and occupied a good deal of my time. To track down the guilty creature, and to determine the mode of its attack on man, was like an exciting piece of detective work. Later on I made this investigation the theme of my thesis for the M.D. degree. This entailed much labour, the collection of material, and the preparation of photographs, drawings, and specimens; in addition to the clinical work. When the treatise was practically finished I had occasion to take, with my wife, one of our long native-boat journeys down the Siang River to Hankow. I took the Thesis with me. It was written on loose sheets of paper, and my object in taking it was to use the long leisure hours of boat travel in revising the manuscript. I did not think of this as a risky thing to do, but as it happened, I very nearly lost the fruit of all my labours.

One night, while at anchor a little distance from the shore, we were visited – not for the first time – by those pests of China's inland waterways, boat thieves.

These gentry usually make their silent raids about 2 a.m. Gliding noiselessly over the water in their flat-bottomed boats, they tie up alongside your craft, using an easy slip-knot for a quick get-away. One of the robbers then creeps aboard, and gains access into the central compartment by skilful removal of one of the shutters. Using only the glow of a stick of incense he quickly collects whatever he finds of value and passes the spoils through the opened shutter to an expectant confrere outside. Money, clocks, and boxes and attaché cases. These, where possible, are passed out bodily.

My wife and I were asleep in our bunks in the adjoining compartment; the crew were in the forward part of the boat, and the skipper in the stern; but we were not awakened. We knew nothing of our night visitors until we rose in the early morning, when objects began to be missed. Many small articles in the living room had vanished. Then I discovered, with horror, that a small unlocked cabin-box, in which for convenience we put the more valued articles of daily use, such as books, writing materials and so on, and in which I kept the thesis, had disappeared. We knew now, of course, that river thieves had paid us a nocturnal visit, and had got clean away with their loot. We could have put up with the deprivation of most of the things, but what caused us real distress was the loss of the precious manuscript. All my work gone in a single night in this senseless manner was insupportable.

I called the skipper and crew, but they, apparently, knew nothing of the robbery. There was nothing to be detected in their stolid physiognomy. It is possible of course that the 'old plank' had been 'squared' on the previous evening; but it would have been impossible to substantiate any suspicions that I may have felt on that score. Only our part of the boat had been invaded.

I went outside to look around. Some discarded articles had been tossed on the roof of the house-boat; but no sign of the box. There was nothing to be seen on the near bank. I told the skipper to cross over to the other side. Here the water was shallow and we had to anchor again a little distance off the land. As the darkness lifted I scanned the fore-shore, and there, in the half-light of early morning, I could see a dark object lying at the water's edge, about 150 yards distant. Presently I made out that it was the box, tumbled over on its side. I hurriedly called to the 'old plank' to have us rowed ashore in the sampan. In a few minutes we were on the spot. At this lonely place the thieves had overhauled their plunder. What they valued they had carried off; but the remainder, for which they had no use, was scattered indiscriminately upon the strand. It was evident that foreign books and papers were not wanted. There was a perfect litter of paper, extending over a considerable area. We discovered at once, to our great relief, that many of the loose sheets were those of the thesis, and eagerly collected these together. Very fortunately it was a perfectly still morning. The papers lay just where they had been strewn. Had there been any wind they must inevitably have been blown into the water and have floated away down stream. We went on collecting and putting the numbered pages together until every sheet had been found. Not one was missing. After this happy recovery the loss of other things did not seem to matter a bit. We returned to our boat and enjoyed a cheerful breakfast after all!

# Chapter XIX

# THE NEW HOSPITAL

As the years passed the medical work grew increasingly heavy. And as the patients came in greater numbers, so our accommodation appeared to shrink in inverse ratio. To find new quarters became an urgent necessity. This need could only be met by the acquisition of additional land.

There was an ample piece of high ground to the rear of our river-front property which was being used for the cultivation of vegetables. The owners were willing to sell, and after prolonged negotiations we finally acquired it. On this fine site it was my ambition to build a new men's hospital, a special department for women, accessory buildings, and a doctor's house. The whole of the foreground property abutting on the native street could be devoted to an extended out-patient practice, while all in-patient work could be carried on in the more retired buildings in the rear.

The realisation of this scheme had, for some time, to be postponed owing to lack of funds. We started a subscription list and quite a big sum was collected from the Chinese themselves. This was supplemented by a generous grant from home. In course of time we had sufficient in hand to meet the estimated cost.

This was my first experience of building. It was a responsible task, but diverting, full of interesting problems. Daily I was in consultation with the head-men, discussing and adjusting difficulties; and I was daily up on the scaffolding inspecting the work. The men were good-humoured and vastly intrigued; but they were also, at times, most exasperating, owing to their easy satisfaction with inferior work. A little deviation

165

from the plumb-line did not matter. It was 'tsa pu to' (near enough); or it was 'mu-yiu fah-toz' [meiyou fazi] (can't be done!)

Building operations occupied many months. Eventually all was complete: a men's hospital for 50 beds, a women's ward for 8 beds, and a doctor's house. The latter was a 2-storied building, with deep verandahs. Attached to this was a fair-sized plot of ground, big enough for a good garden. I planted banana trees; and the land being fertile from years of cultivation suitable plants grew up with surprising rapidity.

The medical work was now well housed, and the new buildings were soon filled to capacity; surgical cases predominating. An English nurse arrived from home to help us; more particularly to take over the matronship of the women's department. The work continued to grow. After 10 years (the 10 years following the Boxer Rising in 1900) it had become fully established, and thousands were treated annually. Ridiculous stories, suspicion, and ill-will were things of the past. On the streets, instead of scowls, we frequently met with smiles. This was the net result after 10 years, and we felt that it had been well worth while.

# Chapter XX

# REVOLUTION

I have already recorded how the Empress-Dowager, accompanied by the deposed Emperor, returned from exile in the autumn of 1901. She reigned for another 7 years in Peking; both she and the Emperor dying almost at the same time in 1908. During that period Her Majesty feeling it politic to yield, to some extent, to the trend of the times had grudgingly sanctioned the introduction of a measure of administrative and educational reform; though this belated repentance did not satisfy the southern provinces.

As, towards the end of this period, i.e. in 1908, the health of Their Majesties had been failing, and as Kwang-Hsu was childless, it became necessary to nominate a successor to the Dragon Throne. The choice of the Dowager had fallen upon Pu-yi, the two year old son of Prince Chun, the Emperor's brother; he who, after the Boxer Rising, had been sent to Europe to apologise to the Kaiser for the German Ambassador, Baron von Ketteler. Immediately upon his nomination the child had been sent for and brought into the Forbidden City. His father was appointed Regent.

The Boy-Emperor, whose Imperial Title was Hsuan-Tung [Xuantong], reigned from the tender age of 2 to that of 6; that is from 1908 to 1912. The Revolution in 1911 was the cause of his enforced abdication in 1912.

It was in the summer of 1911 that I took my family down the Siang [Xiang] and the Yang-tse to Kuling. There was, at that time, a great deal of unrest in the country; indeed the South was seething with discontent. But on this occasion the national resentment was not directed against the foreigner. It was a mass movement, a rebellion, in

167

*Top: Kuling. Postcard from Dr Peake's collection.*

*Bottom: The Peake family home in Kuling.*

which the southern half of the country was mainly involved, against the obsolete government of Peking.

After the death of the Dowager the agitation to sweep away the Manchus and to substitute a Republican form of government had been gathering momentum. At last the smouldering fire burst into flame in the city of Wuchang, the capital of the central province of Hupeh. The Manchu garrison was attacked and overpowered, and the Viceroy's Yamen burnt to the ground. This was the signal for a general uprising of the people, whose hastily mobilised and ill-equipped armies were concentrated in the Wuchang-Hankow area. It was upon this vital nucleus of rebellion that the armed forces of the Imperial Government descended.

Fighting broke out fiercely in and around Hankow. But for neither of the opposing armies was there a competent medical service. On the side of the Revolutionists it was practically non-existent, and doctors were urgently needed.

Leaving Kuling I took passage up-river to join the few doctors in Hankow who were organising aid to the wounded under the Red Cross. On our way we saw grim evidences of the struggle even before we reached our destination. As the steamer approached the city we passed the scene of a recent battle, the dead still lying on the river bank just as they had fallen. Fighting was going on at the time, the rat-tat-tat of the machine guns being plainly audible. Perhaps the most ominous thing of all was the dense column of smoke which ascended from the doomed city, showing that the Imperial troops had already succeeded in setting fire to its out-lying parts.

The Concessions in Hankow were practically deserted by the foreigners; all the women and children, and many of the men, having escaped down river. But there were vast crowds of Chinese who had fled for refuge into the comparative safety of the foreign settlements. They looked dazed, and moved aimlessly along in an unending stream, carrying their babies and pathetic bundles, not knowing where to find shelter or safety.

In the narrow streets of the native city, which adjoined the British area, savage fighting was proceeding – shooting from the houses and around street corners. The situation in the Settlement was not a pleasant one; for although hostilities were not directed against us, bullets were flying freely all over, and anywhere in the open was dangerous.

I made my way through the stupefied crowds to the residence of a friend, and found that his place functioned as the hastily improvised Red Cross Headquarters. There were several doctors there, both British and American, and I received a warm welcome as an addition to the party. It's wonderful what companionship will do in critical situations. I remember that we were a cheerful party, in spite of shells whistling over our heads and bursting in the streets. Many of the houses in the Concession were badly knocked about by shell-fire. Not that there was any intention to damage foreign property; but the opposing armies frequently fired at each other over our heads, and from bad marksmanship we were well peppered.

That evening a large area of the native city was in flames. Viewed from the roof of the Post Office, one of the highest buildings in the Settlement, it was an appalling sight – one continuous line of fire, some three miles in length by about half a mile in width. On three successive nights we watched the conflagration spread, until it appeared that the whole city was aflame.

The only hospitals in Hankow for Chinese patients were the Mission hospitals, and these being situated two on the outskirts of the native city and one in the Concession itself, were mercifully preserved. The furthest was three miles away. Anxiously each night we looked through our glasses, beyond the smoke and the flames, to see if the Red Cross flag was still flying from its roof.

The hospital of the London Mission was only just beyond the Concession boundary. In an incredibly short time it was crowded with wounded. As the fire crept nearer, and the flames threatened the building, we became anxious about the patients lying helpless inside. It seemed only prudent to evacuate them while yet there was time. There were 200 cases to be removed from the beds and floors of a building intended for 60. Having no place to which we could take them we were compelled to put them out in the road. So during the night, while doctors were still operating, stretcher-bearers carried them out and laid them on the pavement. Permission was then obtained

*Hankow burning. Dr Peake's photos
of revolutionary violence, 1911.*

*The aftermath of the revolution in Hankow, 1911,*
*including the ruined Viceroy's house (bottom).*

from the American Episcopal Mission to use their large Church as a hospital ward. The wounded consequently were taken there. We made beds of the pews, turning them face to face and padding them with straw mattresses. They were safe from the fire there at any rate. But then our problems began. Feeding, nursing, sanitation, presented great difficulties. But the hospital staff, and voluntary helpers, rose to the occasion, and ways were found to carry on from day to day. Fortunately it was not for long. Soon after evacuation of the hospital a change in the wind had saved the building, the fire had stopped just short of it, and we were able to move our patients back.

At this time, when the fighting was so fierce, the casualties were very heavy. They poured in faster than we could deal with them. Day and night the booming of the guns filled the air; and in the streets no man, woman, or child was safe from the rifle fire of the soldiers. Even going the short distance to the hospital was dangerous. I can recall now the 'zip' of a bullet as it whizzed past my ear and ricocheted off the brick wall at my side.

The fighting was also very heavy in Han-yang, a city situated a short distance up river. We heard that the Imperialists were attacking just outside the city. As there were no facilities at all in Han-yang for the treatment of the Revolutionary wounded, we organised a recue party with the object of bringing as many as possible into the Settlement. A privately owned steam launch, with Chinese crew, was put at our disposal for this purpose.

Taking surgical requisites we steamed up to Han-yang and established a dressing-station near the river side. News of our arrival quickly spread, and casualties were soon being carried in thick and fast. Many of the wounds were mortal, but some, after receiving first-aid, could be removed to the boat. On that first day our work was very heavy; the launch making three separate trips, and bringing nearly 200 cases to Hankow.

Next day Han-yang was practically in the hands of the Imperial troops. We could not reach the first-aid post without running into the fighting so attended to the casualties that were brought to us by the water-side. Soon bullets began to kick up the dust around us and we felt it wiser to go at once. Very hurriedly we embarked about 30 cases and got away just in the nick of time. In spite of our Red Cross flag we were fired on across the water. One shell pierced the super structure. We heard afterwards that but a few minutes after our getting away the Northerners swung round an angle of the city and rushed down to the water front. Here they found about 1,000 Revolutionaries who had not been able to effect their escape, and these they shot down to a man. We reached the British Settlement in safety.

Soon afterwards there was more to do. The Imperialists, having gained the river banks, kept up a vicious fire at all the sampans on the water. It was hardly possible for a living creature to escape. The occupants, for the most part innocent civilians, fell dead or wounded in their boats; which, without control of any kind, drifted helplessly down stream. So we steamed out again to intercept them, and to rescue any who might still be living. The sight of the dead and dying that met our eyes, as we overhauled one sampan after another, was too awful for description. Most were dead in crouching posture. Many of the boats were semi-swamped in blood and water. An oarsman, shot many times through head and chest, had lurched forwards, but still held the oars in his dead hands. One woman, I remember, had fallen back with a baby held to her breast, one hand covering the infant's head. A bullet had passed through her hand, through the babe's head, and through her chest. Some of the boats were crowded, and consequently were full of corpses. I think we took only five back with us to hospital. One of these we pulled out of the water. He had 8 bullet wounds in his body, and was very far gone, and yet he had managed to slip over the side and to hold on to the boat.

The river was soon cleared of all water-craft, but fighting still continued in certain parts of Hankow which had not been destroyed by fire. One day I ventured up one of those practically deserted streets. Every now and again a rifle-shot would ring out sharply and make one glance round apprehensively. I admit it was foolish to be out in such unhealthy localities, unless for some specific and useful purpose. Some of the sights were horrible. I have a very clear memory of seeing a decapitated head suspended by its pigtail from a charred telegraph pole. Along with the head were several cheap umbrellas and some skeins of

*Decapitated for looting. Hankow, 1911.*

wool. It was evident that this unfortunate had been caught red-handed with his loot, and that drastic retribution had overtaken him on the spot. At the sight of this sickening spectacle I turned back, and was glad to regain unhurt the friendly shelter of the Settlement.

The war was not confined to the Hankow area. Nanking had followed Wuchang, and the city had fallen to the people's army. News reached us of similar successes from other centres in the Yang-tse valley. But Hankow had borne the brunt of the fighting. Nevertheless in spite of the terrible disasters which had overtaken the city – now a scene of ruin and desolation – reinforcements, guns, and munitions kept arriving from the South. The spirit of the people had not been broken. They were, quite obviously, inspired by a high enthusiasm: whereas among the Northern troops, whose pay was constantly in arrears, there was much grumbling and discontent.

Slowly the tide turned. The situation for the Imperialists became more and more embarrassed. Then their rear communications were threatened and orders came from Peking for the retreat. The Northern army melted away. With the defeat of the Government's regular troops, and in the face of the growing military strength of the Southerners, the Peking regime crumpled up. The Imperialist North had yielded to the Revolutionary South. The age-long Monarchical system was dead, and China had become a Republic.

Much excitement followed the victory – which showed itself in a variety of unexpected ways. One morning we woke to find the male population, including our own servants, minus the familiar pigtail; that symbol of subjection to Manchu domination. There was a perfect craze that this gesture of repudiation should be universal. Many who were slow to act were seized in the streets and forcibly relieved of the offending appendage. Following the universal rejoicing there ensued a period of unrest and great confusion. But about the end of the year (1911) Dr Sun Yat-sen, the leading spirit of the Revolutionary movement, returned to China from abroad and was hailed as the first President of the new Republic.

The formal resignation of the Boy-Emperor took place early in the following year (1912); an Abdication Edict being issued under the

Regency. Following this a compromise was effected between Imperial and Republican interests whereby the Royal child was permitted to retain the purely nominal title of 'Emperor', though stripped of every vestige of authority. He was also to be made a grant of 4,000,000 dollars per annum for the up-keep of his court, with its hordes of useless eunuchs; an undertaking 'more honoured in the breach than in the observance'.

So for the next 12 years – that is, between the ages of 6 and 18 – the young Emperor, a very intelligent boy, longing to be outside and to see something of the world, was virtually a prisoner within the walls of the 'Great Within'. His time was spent in serious studies under the guidance of his tutors. This anomalous state of things lasted until 1924, when His Majesty Hsuan-Tung was suddenly divested of his title and emoluments and most unceremoniously forced to vacate the Forbidden City. He retired as a private citizen to Tientsin. In 1931 he returned, the last scion of his dynasty, to the land of his Imperial ancestors, Manchuria.

It would be profitless to follow the intricacies, contentions, and rivalries which marked the change-over from a monarchical to a Republican form of Government. There had indeed been misrule and injustice, bribery and corruption, under the old autocracy, but at least law and order had, in the main, been preserved. Such administrative chaos and disorganisation marked the birth-pangs of the new dispensation that many of us foreign on-lookers were inclined to think it was a case of 'out of the frying pan into the fire'; and to wonder if, after all, the ancient absolutism was not more in accordance with the temperament and character of the Chinese people.

President Sun Yat-sen was followed in 1913 by Yuan Shi-K'ai, former Provincial Governor and Grand Councillor under the Empress-Dowager; and Commander-in-Chief of the army. He was at heart a staunch supporter of the Imperial tradition. Thinking he could rely on the loyalty of his troops he undertook the Presidency with the secret aim of restoring the Monarchy. He hoped to found a new Dynasty, with himself as the first Emperor; and in this project he could count on considerable support in the North. But his plans were constantly frustrated by the Japanese, who stirred up the opposition of the Kuomintang, or Republican Party. Japan had designs of her own. She was glad to see the country torn and distracted, and the last thing she desired was a consolidated China, established again on the old model, and under the dictatorship of this strong man.

It was about this time that I arrived up north to take over the medical work of my Society in Tientsin, and had the honour, with some other foreign doctors, of being presented to His Excellency Yuan-Shi-K'ai in Peking. He struck me as being a very worried and a very sick man. But though his difficulties increased he actually *did* ascend the Throne, reigning for a very brief period – a matter of days. Ultimately he renounced the throne, and died shortly afterwards, a disappointed and broken man.

After the death of Yuan-Shi-K'ai the affairs of the State became hopelessly disorganised and power passed into the hands of military Governors of the Provinces, the so-called 'War Lords'. These unscrupulous and rapacious individuals, taking advantage of China's chaotic condition and their own military strength, seized their opportunity to batten on the people and to amass huge fortunes for themselves. Iniquitous taxes were imposed; and large revenues were raised from the enforced cultivation of opium in place of rice. There was much quarrelling and fighting among themselves – levying troops for their wars by the most callous press-gang methods. Owing to their grievances, and particularly to the non-payment of their wages, soldiers deserted in large numbers. These roamed the country as armed brigands, terrorising and plundering the people.

After years of turmoil and civil war some semblance of unity emerged under the leadership of Chiang Kai-shek.[37] Under his military leadership and guidance vital reconstruction was taking place, and the country was making real progress, when Japan struck her treacherous blow. To the Land of the Rising Sun a strong China was anathema.

---

37 [FW] Some of Peake's enthusiasm for Chiang Kai-shek (1887–1975) may derive from the fact that Chiang's third wife, Song Meiling, was a Christian, and Chiang is said to have converted in order to marry her. They started the 'New Life Movement' in 1934, in which Confucianism, Christianity and nationalism were invoked to rally support for the Kuomintang in its struggle against the Communists.

She must strike, and strike quickly. A few months at the outside would suffice to bring China to her knees. That would be a mere 'incident' for her soaring ambitions did not end there. For many years Japan had dreamed of conquest extending over the whole of Eastern Asia, including the East Indies, Australia, and even India. It was becoming urgent to finish off China first. Japan's action had aroused in her a latent patriotism unsuspected by her best friends. It had galvanised her to heights of fierce resistance, which came as a shock and a most unpleasant surprise to the arrogant Aggressor, and it unified the country as nothing else could have done.

I am writing this in the ninth year of the war, and the Japanese are further removed than ever from the accomplishment of their grandiose designs. China still fights heroically under the same great leader, Generalissimo Chiang Kai-shek.

And the end is not in doubt. This is doubly assured, for since Japan struck at China in 1936 she now has ranged against her the additional might of the Anglo-Saxon race. China will emerge victorious, and the high qualities of her people, dormant for so long but now quickened to a new life, ensure for her a great and honourable future.

Top: Dr Peake's assistant in Tientsin, Dr Lei.

Bottom: Mervyn Peake, aged about 1, with Dr Lei's infant son.

# Chapter XXI

# THE HOSPITAL AT TIENTSIN

It was after the cessation of hostilities in Hankow that I returned to Hunan for the last time. My right-hand man, Dr Lei, had been in charge of the hospital during my absence and had carried on the work with characteristic ability. But our object in returning was not to pick up the threads again but, on the contrary, to wind up our affairs, pack up our goods, and bid farewell to our Chinese friends. The work of the hospital was not being discontinued. It was merely being transferred to an American Society, and this transference carried with it the prospect of larger financial support, and an increased medical staff. I myself had been assigned to the Mackenzie Memorial Hospital in Tientsin [Tianjin], which was at that time without a Medical Superintendent.

The long journey to the far north, undertaken late in 1912, occupied exactly one month. It entailed considerable hardship. We slipped down the Siang River in our house-boat in comparative comfort, but were held up in the Tung-ting Lake by a northerly gale. It was bitterly cold, though we found a degree of shelter in the lee of a sandbank. There we held fast. We had of course brought provisions for the river journey with us; but had not anticipated such a serious delay. The food problem became acute. Fortunately one of the last things which had been thrown on board when we left was a case of condensed milk, and this just saved the situation for our infant son.

When the storm had abated we made our way slowly across the water to the town of Yo-chow on the north side of the lake, and there we found a small steam-tug about to start on its return journey to Hankow. Loaded up as we were with furniture and household goods we could not transfer to this tiny steamer, but the Chinese skipper readily consented to tow us. Thus the last stage down the Yang-tse was completed in record time. The remainder of our journey north from Hankow to Peking, and then on to Tientsin, was accomplished by rail.

We found the North very different from the Central and Southern regions. It was evident at once that we had left behind us the China of the picture books and had reached instead a dry and weary land.

But Peking, the ancient Capital, which had been rebuilt on such a magnificent scale by Kublai Khan in the 13th century, fascinated me. The early glories of the city have been glowingly described by Marco Polo, who, as an honoured guest at the Court of the great Mongol Emperor, had ample opportunities of exploring its many wonders.

The ground plan, as designed by Kublai, is rectangular, the streets running in parallel lines from North to South and from East to West. The city forms a perfect square, enclosed within massive battlemented walls and colossal gateways; each side of the square being four miles in length. This is known as the Manchu or Tartar City.

Within the Tartar City, like a square within a square, is the Imperial City, itself surrounded by high walls over six miles in circumference. A chain of artificial lakes extends right through the Imperial City, and grouped about these lakes are the spacious residences and gardens of the High Mandarins and Princes. Within the Imperial City again is the centrally placed and closely guarded Forbidden City, the 'Great Within'; which itself is protected by imposing purple-coloured walls over two miles in extent. This secluded Enclosure contained the resplendent yellow-tiled palaces of the 'Son of Heaven'.

I was given, with some others, the special opportunity of entrance into the Forbidden City and of viewing the beautiful palaces, lotus lakes, and temples. Crossing the marble bridges we visited the lonely island on which the unhappy Emperor had been kept so close a prisoner.

The enforced abdication of the Boy-Emperor had taken place shortly before our visit, and we were not escorted, of course, to that sequestered quarter of the Forbidden City where his greatly reduced Court had functioned, but an air of sadness and desolation pervaded

*The Temple of Heaven (top) and the grounds of the Summer Palace (bottom), Peking, photographed by Dr Peake.*

*Traditional means of transport in Peking.*

the whole place. No life stirred within the deserted precincts. It was plain that the glory had departed.

In the Tartar City – intended originally for Manchu residence only but now occupied also by numerous Chinese – we were free to go about as we pleased. The distances are great, but rickshaws were plentiful. The streets I found much broader than in the southern cities, and full of unfamiliar traffic: the mule-drawn Peking cart, and the long strings of camels from the deserts of Mongolia, struck a novel note. Many of the shop-fronts were flamboyantly decorated, some displaying a perfect riot of ornate carving and gilding.

Some of China's most sacred buildings are situated in the north-eastern corner of the Tartar City; notably the beautiful Temple erected to the memory of Confucius, the Hall of the Classics, and the Lama Temple. The latter was said to have over 1,000 officiating priests. The Buddha is 90 feet high and 36 feet broad: a huge gilded monster, with a lotus plant growing out of its right arm. Ten thousand images of Buddha fill the niches round the gallery.

Essentially Peking is composed of two cities in close juxtaposition, the Manchu and the Chinese. When you have passed through the Chien Men [Qian men], that is, the great main gate in the centre of the south wall of the Tartar City, you are in the Chinese city. The latter is oblong in shape and is surrounded by a great wall which has a mileage nearly equal to that of its neighbour.

This is the animated business part of Peking – pulsating with life – a veritable hive of unresting industry. Foreigners love to go shopping in this area, for the great store-houses are crammed full of the most delectable wares – curios, objets d'art, porcelains, cloisonné, silks, embroideries and choice velvets. This is a region par excellence for exploration: but hands must be kept resolutely in one's pockets! I confess, however, to having fallen victim to a beautiful fawn and blue carpet, which has now been in use for over 30 years.

But the Chinese city is not given over entirely to trade. In its southernmost part are two large park-like areas. One of these contains the far-famed Temple of Heaven. Here the 'Son of Heaven' was wont annually to sacrifice, with elaborate ritual, for the sins of his people.

The other encloses the Temple of Agriculture, where the Emperor, having sacrificed to the spirits of the Harvest, handled the plough and cut the first furrow in honour of Husbandry and by way of encouraging its pursuit among his subjects.

There was very little to refresh the eye as we looked from our carriage window travelling by rail between Peking and Tientsin. Both these great cities, and hundreds of towns and villages around them, are situated in a flat, dusty plain. Periodically, as we discovered later, north-westerly gales, laden with the fine sand of the Gobi desert, sweep over this vast territory, darkening the sky as by a great pall of yellow fog. These 'dust-storms' are a trial to everybody. Your 'boy' in particular curses them for the extra work they give him. He closes your shutters and your double windows (necessitating the use of artificial light everywhere), he blocks up every chink and crevice, and still the dust pours in. Very quickly everything in the house is thickly covered. The fine sand penetrates into your clothes, into your hair, into your eyes, ears, and nose, and grits between your teeth. It was a new experience, something we never had to contend with in the damp, green regions of the South.

Tientsin itself, situated about 70 miles to the south-east of Peking, is one of the great trading centres of the East. It is some 40 miles from the sea, but ships reach the port by steaming up the Pei-ho [Beihe], or North River; a mere stream when compared with the Yang-tse, but deep enough for foreign vessels coming in on the tide. The ancient native city has a population of over a million crowded within its narrow streets; and clustered outside it are the foreign Concessions – British, French and Russian, each administered by its own local authorities. In the Chinese city you will see only Chinese, but on the wide thoroughfares of the Settlements, though the Chinese predominate, you will also meet people from all over the wide world – Europeans, Americans, Japanese, Indians, Burmese, Annamese – going about their business on foot, in motor cars, horse-carriages, and rickshaws; all the congested traffic being controlled by trained native police.

One of the busiest avenues of traffic in Tientsin, running from the native city and through the foreign quarter, is known as the Taku [Dagu] Road; and it is on this road that the hospital to which I had

Street life in Peking.

been appointed is situated. The hospital has a long and honourable history. The commencement of the medical work goes back as far as 1860 when a British Expeditionary Force was sent to China to compel the observance of Treaty obligations. The Taku Forts at the mouth of the North River were taken, the expedition made its way upriver to Tientsin, and thence overland by forced marches to Peking. A garrison was located in Tientsin.

I once had in my possession a very old and faded document entitled 'Report on a Hospital for the Treatment of Sick Chinese; established by the British Army of Occupation, Jan 11th 1861'. Thus, very soon after their arrival in the place we find the Army authorities commencing medical work for the benefit of the people with whom they were supposed to be in a state of war. The writer of the report commences as follows:

A good opportunity of extending the benefits of European Medicine and Surgery to the inhabitants of North China having offered by the circumstances of a British Force being quartered in Tientsin, the Commandant of the troops was in the early part of January of the present year (1861) consulted upon the practicability of establishing a hospital for this purpose. Brig-Gen. Stavely entered most cordially into the scheme. Under his orders a Committee was formed with a view to carrying out the preliminary details, and to conduct the affairs of the intended Institution; he himself agreeing to act as the Treasurer.

We then find the following interesting reference to Gen. Gordon,[38] who was then with the Force as a Captain in the Royal Engineers.

---

38 [FW] General Charles Gordon (1833–1885) of the Royal Engineers arrived in China in 1860 and laid out the boundary of the British concession in Tientsin, where the municipal hall (which has only recently been demolished) was named Gordon Hall in his honour. He then left for Shanghai, where he joined the 'Ever Victorious Army' raised by Li Hung-chang [Li Hongzhang] to fight the Taiping rebels who were defeated in 1864. He was killed at Khartoum in Sudan.

A suitable building having been engaged at a monthly rent, Capt. Gordon was so good as to superintend the fitting-up of it; separate portions were prepared for the reception of male and female patients; a kitchen was arranged; an apartment furnished as a surgery; servants engaged; an agreement made with a native contractor for the supply of all ordinary articles of food and fuel; and these arrangements completed, notices printed in Chinese were placarded throughout the city intimating that on the 23rd of January the hospital was to be formally opened.

This work, conducted with the aid of an interpreter by the medical officers of the B.E.F., turned out a great success. Much sickness and suffering was relieved. But in the same year the Force was withdrawn, and the undertaking had to close down.

It was not until 1868 that the medical work was revived by the London Missionary Society. In those early years the services of any and every well-disposed doctor was requisitioned, even the gun-boat surgeons doing their bit. But since the year 1879 the London Missionary Society have appointed their own physicians to the charge of the work.

Dr J. Mackenzie arrived in the Spring of that year. His skill as a surgeon soon became widely known. Owing to his successful attendance on Lady Li, wife of H.E. the Viceroy Li Hung-chang, he sprang at once into prominence. He became physician to His Excellency, and succeeded in enlisting his sympathy and help in the work of the hospital.

It is told how on one occasion the Viceroy requested the Doctor to perform a surgical operation in the courtyard of his Yamen so that he and his official subordinates might witness for themselves something of the wonders of Western surgery. This was accordingly done. On the day set for this great occasion the Viceroy and his concourse of satellites, dressed in their full regalia, took their places in the arena. There, in the centre of this court and before this curious assembly, Mackenzie, having made all necessary preparation beforehand, and having his anaesthetist and assistants with him, proceeded with the performance of several spectacular operations, including the removal of a tumour the size of a human head growing from the back of a man's neck. Surely never

*The Mission hospital at Tientsin.*

before or since has a surgeon conducted his work amid such strange surroundings, or in so dramatic a setting!

Needless to say the reputation of the doctor and his hospital were made. From that time patients crowded to him in such numbers that it became impossible for him to overtake the work. Not only in Tientsin but also far into the surrounding country, the hospital is still known as the 'Ma-tai-fu-i-yuan', that is, 'The Dr Mackenzie Hospital'.

In his promise to Mackenzie that he would give him practical support the Viceroy was as good as his word. Indeed, it was he who supplied the funds necessary for the erection of a new Out-patient Department. This took the form of an attractive building in the Taku Road, entirely in Chinese style, with a roof of richly-coloured glazed tiles, the whole weighty superstructure being supported by massive and heavily lacquered wooden pillars.

This was the hospital to which I had been transferred. It was evident from the first that the new work presented problems of an entirely different character from those with which I had had to contend in the south. Those had been pioneering days in the far interior, but here was an old established work in a Treaty Port, and in one of China's biggest cities. Its history took one back over half a century. But, unhappily, it had latterly fallen upon evil times. The English doctor who had been in charge had resigned two years previously owing to ill-health in his family, and the medical work in the interim had been carried on by a Western-trained Chinese physician.

Our first acquaintance with the hospital was depressing in the extreme. It did not require much insight to perceive that things had got in a very bad way. The old buildings were in a poor state of repair. The premises were not even clean. The staff had become completely demoralised, and in consequence the work itself had dwindled to a low ebb. There were very few in-patients in the place, and out-patients had fallen to a mere trickle. The reputation of the hospital, once so high, had suffered badly.

What accounted for this deterioration? The chief cause was the lack of foreign supervision. The qualified Chinese doctor who was acting as locum tenens had turned out a failure. The ease with which money could be extracted from the patients had proved too big a temptation. Drugs, the property of the hospital, were secretly sold for his own private gains. The poorer patients were treated with discourtesy, and discipline had gone to pieces. Everyone, in a big, or little way was 'on the make'. It was evident that most of them would have to go. A fresh start had to be made, and in order to do this it was advisable to close the hospital for a couple of months. During this time urgently needed repairs could be carried out.

But the direful thing about the dismissal of hospital assistants in China is that they resume private life as medical practitioners, advertising their high qualifications as having been 'trained' at the hospital. The ex-assistant, perhaps formerly but a probationer attendant in the surgery, will gaily attempt to reproduce what he has seen. He has seen the Doctor open an abscess on many occasions. The Doctor just takes a knife and cuts right into it, and out flows the pus, and the patient soon gets well. It is all so very simple. He could do that too. Why not? But 'a little knowledge is a dangerous thing'. All swellings are not abscesses, and he is apt to thrust his knife in the wrong place. In one case, our enterprising young friend, lacking proper instruments, used an oily pair of scissors (used for trimming the lamp wick) to open a swelling in the groin. But his luck was out; the swelling was not due to an abscess but to a hernia. Disdaining antiseptic precautions, or the use of an anaesthetic, the crude implement was made to cut through the skin and right into the bowel; with, of course, rapidly fatal consequences. Such occurrences resulting from dismissal were not, however, within our power to control.

On re-opening the hospital the number of patients attending the out-patient clinic was not great. But it steadily increased. During the summer, six months after the re-start, the daily attendance was over one hundred. As our waiting-room accommodation was limited, and as the numbers still increased, many had to sit on the stone steps outside, from whence they overflowed down to the street gate. Although Dr Lei and I worked over-time, we could not adequately overhaul the crowds of sick humanity with which we were daily confronted.

Carrying patients to
the Mission hospital.

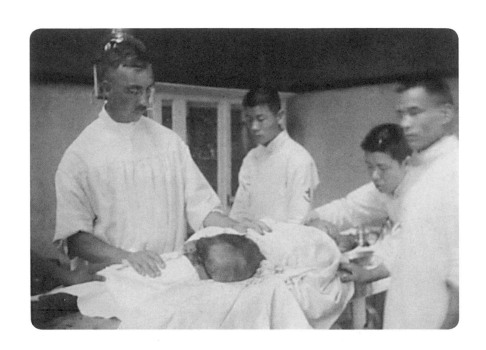

The staff at the Mission hospital.

# Chapter XXII

# THE DAILY ROUND

We had arrived in Tientsin in the winter and at once ran into such bitter weather as we had never before experienced. This was not surprising since we had come 1,000 miles further north. The temperature was down to many degrees below freezing point (often it was below zero) and it remained down throughout the winter months – so that there was, both day and night, a continuous hard frost. The river, in spite of the strong current, froze over with rough ice several feet in thickness and became a highway of sledges.[39] Even the sea was frozen for some distance from the coast. The piercing cold of the north winds, coming from the arctic regions across Siberia, cut through one like a knife. Fur caps with ear-flaps, and fur coats, were general, and we found them a necessity. The air was very dry and very invigorating, a complete opposite to the humid, enervating climate of the south. Early in the year, however, almost suddenly, the cold passed and gave way to a warmth which rapidly progressed to an intense heat, everything up to 100°F in the shade, and sometimes over.

Soon after reopening the hospital it became apparent that the vast majority of our cases were of a surgical nature. In Tientsin, where the ground had been broken for so many years, patients consented to operation with the greatest readiness. Their confidence in Western surgery was supreme, and they willingly took whatever risks might be

---

39 [ECP] The ice is dug out by the native ice-merchants, who store it underground, packed around with straw. They drive a lucrative trade by selling it during the hot summer. It is however very impure and not fit for consumption, though useful for other purposes.

involved. This greatly reduced one's anxiety and responsibility. There was no fear of any kind of trouble even if a case should terminate fatally.

Operative work was routine every morning and was often very heavy. During my last year in China the number of operations under general anaesthetic exceeded 1,200.

For all these patients we had a plan by which selected cases were allowed to return home in the evening. They rested in the hospital during the day, and by night-time, when they had recovered from the first effects of the anaesthetic, they were taken home. They could later attend as out-patients. In this way many cases could obtain treatment quickly when the alternative would have been to send them away for lack of beds. This, to English ears, may sound a very drastic procedure, but, used with discretion, the method worked perfectly well with the hardier and more phlegmatic patients with whom we had to deal. Inured to a hard life they bore pain well and were most uncomplaining. Moreover they took chloroform well, and we did not have to compete with post-anaesthetic vomiting, nor do I remember a single case where a fatal issue resulted from the use of chloroform.[40]

It may be of interest to say something of the nature of the work carried on in the hospital, so different in its oriental setting, from what we are accustomed to at home. The record of a few concrete cases will perhaps best illustrate this.

Sudden and serious emergencies, often of an unusual character, frequently intruded upon our normal routine. This was a prominent feature; something which I had not had to deal with in Hunan. It was not difficult to account for this. In Heng-chow we had lived in a purely native city, living its own leisurely life as it had for centuries, and untouched by the hustle of modern industrial activity. But life was a very different thing in the foreign settlements of Tientsin. Here the dense wheeled traffic in the streets, the machinery of the travelling firms, the tramways, and the railway trains were all things to which multitudes of the Chinese had not yet become accustomed. They were

---

40 [ECP] We did not use ether at all: it is too volatile a liquid. Evaporation from the open mask is so rapid in the heat that to get a patient thoroughly narcotised presented real difficulty.

196

unused to foreign ways, seemed to be quite unaware of danger, and were incredibly careless.

Many urgent cases reached us from the streets, others from the factories using machinery, with which employees had a happy knack of getting mixed up. Mangled hands, from being caught in the wheels; crushed feet, from falling weights; foreign bodies in the eye; severe burns and scalds, were common injuries.

There were still many in the north who had not discarded the pigtail, and this appendage, hanging freely down the back, was apt to get them in trouble. I remember one man being brought in with his scalp turned inside out and lying over his face. His queue had been caught in the cogs of revolving machinery and the whole scalp had been stripped forward from the back of his head to the eye-brows, exposing the bare skull. After disinfection it was replaced and stitched in position. He healed up perfectly and without complication.

But by far the most serious casualties were brought in from the railway. Passengers would leap from fast-moving trains, evidently expecting to land quite comfortably on their feet. Broken heads or mangled limbs were the consequence.

During out-patient clinic on one occasion a woman was carried in from the railway. She was pulse-less, and suffering from severe shock and haemorrhage. What was the history? Being a day of blazing heat, and seeing some trucks in a siding near the station, she had crept under one of them for the sake of its grateful shade. She lay down with her legs over the line and went to sleep. While she slept an engine reversed into the siding, coupled on to the trucks, and drew out. Both limbs were over-run and crushed. There was no one to apply 'first-aid', but she was hoisted into a rickshaw and brought round. The clinic was interrupted and the patient carried to the operating room. After injections of morphine and intravenous saline solution the patient rallied but both legs had to be amputated. She made a hard fight for life, but succumbed after nearly a fortnight.

Even though our space was so limited casualties were sometimes thrust upon us. Such was the case of a man who was completely paralysed in the lower half of his body as the result of fracture of the spine, due to a fall from some high scaffolding. He was carried to an inn, where he remained for a few days – presumably until his means were exhausted. The inn-keeper then finding him a burden paid a rickshaw man to remove him and dump him somewhere. He was duly deposited in a ditch on the outskirts of the city, and left to his fate. How long he remained there I do not remember, but he was ultimately rescued by a foreigner, who, passing along the road above and hearing a call for help, stopped to investigate. Being acquainted with the language he had no difficulty in understanding the poor fellow's appeal, which was that the stranger would come down and strangle him. Instead he had him lifted out and brought to the hospital. The case was a hopeless one, and he died a few days after admission.

Severe head injuries, with fractured skulls, were not uncommon. Speaking from memory I would say that such cases were more numerous than broken arms and legs. The case of a man who had fallen from a height is typical. He was brought in insensible, but soon recovered consciousness. It was then found that he had no power to move the right leg. The skull had been fractured and a piece of bone on the left side of the head had been driven inwards. It was the pressure of this fragment on the brain that accounted for the paralysis of the leg. When the pressure had been relieved by levering the depressed bone up into position the patient rapidly recovered.

Another case, which ended fatally, was that of a man who had been brought in from the railway. This was at a time when attempts were being made to put a stop to the illegal traffic in opium. In order to escape from the police inspector, who was on board and searching the passengers, he had jumped from the train while it was in rapid motion. We found about 1 lb of the crude drug, contained in a pig's bladder, on his person.

Bone affections due to disease, mainly tubercular, were very common, and the joints were most frequently attacked. When taken in time useful limbs could be restored, but patients frequently came too late. Sometimes it was difficult to decide whether immediate amputation was indicated, or whether an attempt should be made to save the limb. In a prolonged effort to save a leg one might lose the life.

I recall now the case of a small boy of twelve, suffering from advanced tubercular disease of the knee. On account of famine in his district his father, being unable to support him any longer, had turned him away from home to fend for himself. He had come to Tientsin to beg; sleeping at night in some kind of shelter which he had found near the railway station. At last unable to get about any longer he was brought to the hospital. We found the joint completely disorganised and full of pus. His general condition was very bad. It was a clear case for amputation. He made a quick recovery and was soon getting about on crutches. He turned out a bright, intelligent boy and was soon learning to read. We felt we could not send him out on the streets again. The plan was to apprentice him to some kind of sedentary occupation, such as tailoring, and I think that is what eventually happened.

Take another instance, where we ventured to treat the case conservatively. The patient, in this case a man, was desperately ill and near his end. He was found in the street by some well-meaning person, who, wishing, as the Chinese say, 'to accumulate merit' and add to his credit account in the world to come, had directed a rickshaw coolie to take him off to the 'Dr Mackenzie Hospital'.

The rickshaw man, having deposited his fare at our front gate, very naturally made off. Here he was later discovered and brought inside. An operation to open up the joint was done at once, affording great relief from pain and fever. He remained in hospital over three months, and on leaving, fat and well, was provided with a new out-fit of clothes, and with sufficient money to pay his travelling expenses back to his own people in the country, from whom, as a sort of 'prodigal son', he had originally run away. We hoped we had, in a double sense, succeeded in in putting him on his feet, when, a few weeks later, he turned up again in the clinic, not having made any attempt to return home, and once more in rags, for he had pawned his good clothes for 80 cents, less than 2/.

Occasionally operations were required for the correction of deformities resulting from injuries. A strange case was that of a man who came to the hospital on crutches with his right leg dislocated at the knee and bent backwards at a right angle. It was stiff and fixed in that position.

There was a scar at the top of the shin bone in front but the limb was not diseased, and the cause of the deformity was obscure. No history could be elicited from the patient, and I possessed no X-ray facilities. In operating to give him a straight leg I had to saw through the bone, and in doing so encountered unexpected resistance. On completing the section I discovered that I had sawn through a large leaden shrapnel bullet. Only after this was the patient willing to explain that he had been in the fighting in Hankow during the Revolution. A bullet had struck him below the knee and bent his leg backwards. After that he could not straighten it. He did not know the bullet was still in the leg.

Not all our cases were from the city. Serious casualties were brought in also from the country. These were nearly always the work of discontented soldiers who had deserted from the armies of the contending war-lords. At the time of which I write roving bands of these armed brigands scoured the country, battening themselves on the villages until a sufficient sum could be collected from the inhabitants to buy them off. Frequently they would break into the better houses or farmsteads, looting and demanding silver. If resistance was offered the answer would be a bullet, or the thrust of a bayonet. By the time such cases reached us, having been jolted for days in coolie-borne litters, they were in a shocking condition. Some, as one always finds in war surgery, had narrow escapes. One such case had received a bayonet thrust in the chest, just missing the heart, but resulting in protracted illness from empyema. In another the bullet had entered between the ear and the eye, and there was no exit wound. We daily awaited the development of serious symptoms, but nothing transpiring we had to discharge him. He went off merrily, carrying with him his souvenir in the shape of a bullet lodged in the base of his skull.

In the case of attacks upon the more wealthy, if ready money was not available upon demand, a favourite procedure with the brigands was to seize one of the family, preferably a male child, and carry him off. A big sum would be exacted for the return of the hostage. It was often with the greatest difficulty that the ransom could be found – not to speak of the heart-rending distress caused to the family.

Callous indifference and cruelty were characteristic traits of these ruthless ruffians. A particularly revolting instance of this was reported to me. Having broken into a well-to-do home in the usual manner, and the large sum of money demanded not being forthcoming, a small boy was seized and carried off pending the payment of the ransom. The parents and relatives were only able to raise half the amount, in return for which the gangsters, as a grim jest, returned half the boy!

Abdominal operations were becoming more frequent when I left China, owing to the fact that patients consulted us earlier, and before it was too late. Appendicitis, in my experience, was not a common complaint. But hernia was frequently encountered. These cases were often of long-standing and the patients quite incapacitated. From being the bread-winners of the family they were reduced to dependence upon their relatives. From the economic point of view alone, therefore, the operation was well worth while. Apart from this aspect of the question these patients were always in danger of serious complications which threatened life.

Among the abdominal conditions which I found were more frequently met with in China than at home were stone in the bladder and tropical abscess of the liver, the latter the aftermath of amoebic dysentery. Stone is the cause of a great deal of suffering. One of my patients suffered with such excruciating pain that that he was on the verge of suicide. In this case I removed a large rough stone, the size of a goose's egg, which turned the scale at half-a-pound. I still have it in my possession.

A doctor cannot long be in a hospital amongst the Chinese without being struck by the high proportion of patients suffering from different kinds of tumours, both innocent and malignant. Some of these reach monstrous proportions, such as we never see in England, where relief is sought so much earlier. Operations for the removal of these 'growths' had frequently to be undertaken. One case of a large growth on the upper jaw comes to my mind. Dr Lei and I were not disposed to tackle the operation, fearing the patient would die from uncontrollable haemorrhage and from shock, but as he and his relations were very importunate we were persuaded to undertake it. As soon as the patient was under anaesthetic tracheotomy was performed so that he could breathe through the tube in his wind-pipe. This enabled us to pack the throat with gauze and so prevent blood from being aspirated into the lungs. Next the large blood vessel in the neck, known as the carotid artery, was tied; thus cutting off the main blood supply to the tumour. With these preliminary precautions the whole growth, with that part of the jaw to which it was attached, was removed without much difficulty and with very little bleeding. The patient made a good recovery.

Sometimes operations were required for some pathological condition affecting the blood vessels. I gained the impression that varicose veins of the leg were not so frequently encountered as in this country, but that might be because Chinese patients would not be likely to seek advice except in very aggravated cases. My first case of this trouble soon after our arrival in Tientsin was that of a eunuch from Peking whose veins were in such a bad condition that according to his account, the foreign doctors in Peking had declined to operate. He expressed the likely opinion that his duties at the Palace, where he was constantly kept standing in attendance upon the Boy-Emperor, accounted for the very advanced degree of his trouble. We noticed, after operations, that he seemed more than usually grateful. One Sunday morning, some time after he had left us, he reappeared at the head of a procession at the hospital gates. A blare of trumpets proclaimed his arrival, while his retinue, in the quaintest of liveries bore aloft a gaudy complimentary tablet.[41]

In the Mackenzie Memorial Hospital in my time we had no regular beds for women, though we had to deal with emergencies as they arose. There was, however, a Mission hospital for female patients in the native city run by American women-doctors, and I was privileged to operate on my serious cases there. These were mainly maternity patients where, owing to complications, it was necessary to resort to Caesarean section. On one of these cases I was called upon to perform this operation for the second time in the following year. The mother did well on both occasions, and both the children, a boy and a girl, were saved.

---

41 [ECP] Complimentary scrolls and tablets were sometimes presented by the more well-to-do patients to express their gratitude, and to pay the most embarrassingly eulogistic compliments!

Though the work of the hospital (both for in- and out-patients) was predominantly surgical, it was by no means exclusively so. Lung tuberculosis was rampant. In the South I had always found tubercular disease very prevalent, but in the North it seemed to be even more rife. The reason for the wide-spread distribution of this scourge is to be found firstly in the overcrowding which results from the national custom of keeping the ever-growing family as much as possible under one roof. When the sons marry they bring their wives into the old ancestral home. More children are born, who, in their turn, grow up and marry; the sons remaining at home, the daughters compelled to start a new life in the home of her husband. Of course the aged drop off at the top as the young come on at the bottom, but as the latter marry early there are frequently four generations at a time in the home. Then if tuberculosis is introduced the infection spreads rapidly. Not understanding the infectious nature of the malady there is no attempt at what we would consider the most elementary precautions.

It was in my first summer in Tientsin that I discovered that tropical diseases were by no means absent from North China. In spite of the cold winters the summers were exceedingly hot. Malaria, both the benign and malignant types, I found to be common. Microscopic examination of blood films showed the parasite in all its forms. The periodically recurring attacks of ague, every third or fourth day, which occur in the benign forms of the disease, make the diagnosis easy; but in malignant malaria the symptoms may be very misleading. In the case of a child of two, who was gravely ill, the clinical picture was that of dysentery. There was no response to anti-dysenteric treatment. Blood examination revealed no parasites, but a count of the white cells pointed to a malarial origin. Intra-muscular injections of quinine were given in full doses. Steady improvement set in at once, and we had the satisfaction of seeing the child progress to complete recovery.

Obscure fevers are very common in the tropics. Here again the microscope is our court of appeal: indeed, it is a good rule to examine the blood in every case of fever the nature of which is not perfectly clear. In such cases the diagnosis is always greatly facilitated, and often may become at once apparent. This is strikingly the case in Relapsing

Fever, where a stained film will reveal the parasite known as spirillum; an elongated and undulating protozoon which lives and moves freely in the blood plasma.

Tropical dysentery, due to infection by the amoeba coli was common; and another tropical condition known as Kala-azar was widely prevalent among the village children. In this terrible disease the microscopic parasite abounds in prodigious numbers in the spleen, which becomes enormously enlarged. The mortality in untreated cases must be well nigh 100%. The father of one of the children treated at the hospital told me that the Chinese in his locality had their own method of attempting a cure. He informed me that occasionally, when a child died of Kala-azar, the abdomen was opened and the big diseased spleen removed from the body. It was then cut up into bits, dried before a fire, and made up into little pellets to be administered in small doses to other children afflicted by the same malady. If the diseased organ had been removed from a boy this extraordinary medicament is said to be only efficacious for a girl; but when removed from a girl it must be administered only to boys. The father related how his own child had been dosed in this manner; but he could not speak enthusiastically of the treatment. It was certainly the first time that I had heard of the Chinese removing diseased organs post mortem and compounding them into a medicine for the cure of the identical disease in others.[42] But in the light of our modern methods of vaccine therapy is there not a germ of truth in the idea?

My cases were nearly always in children. I can recall only one case in an adult, that of a Korean student who was studying in Tientsin. This youth was arrested by the Japanese on the charge of being implicated in anti-Japanese activities when in Korea. The charge was unfounded (and could not later be substantiated) but the poor fellow was dragged off to Seoul, where he was imprisoned and tortured to make confession concerning things about which he was completely ignorant. He was later released and returned to Tientsin. He got back, however, only

---

42 [ECP] In this connection another strange practice is the treatment sometimes resorted to in the case of mad-dog bite, when some hair from the dog is taken and bound into the wound.

to die in hospital; for on arrival I found him suffering from Kala-azar which he had contracted while a prisoner. Before his death he gave me an account of his exile, and of the sufferings and indignities endured at the hands of the Japanese in Korea.

It was evident then, even during my first summer in North China, that there was still ample scope for investigation into those complaints which are peculiar to the tropics. I had not long to wait before obscure cases, exhibiting signs and symptoms very similar to those of Kala-azar, presented themselves. As in the latter disease, there was extreme weakness, anaemia, and irregular fever. There was also a dropsical condition of the lower half of the body. But it was the adults who were chiefly affected, and not the children; and the physical examination revealed enlargement of the liver and not of the spleen. In advanced cases this organ was enormously swollen, bulging forward from under the ribs to an extraordinary degree, and giving the patient's abdomen a characteristic appearance, being so much greater above than below. But the chief feature was the discovery in the blood of these cases of a flagellated parasite, free in the blood plasma, and showing astonishing motility and vitality. Using the most powerful lens of our microscope Dr Lei and I were able to detect the parasite in fresh blood withdrawn direct from the liver. Sometimes, when the fever was on, it was present in such enormous numbers that the blood seemed positively alive. In size it varied from young forms which gave the impression of being almost beyond microscopic range, to large ones half the diameter of a red blood corpuscle. The smaller ones were the more actively mobile, but occasionally we came across one of the large forms, lashing out with its flagella for all the world like a miniature octopus.

I showed the parasite to several other men, who all expressed their astonishment, and their agreement with me that it was new. I wrote articles on the subject for the *China Medical Journal* and for the *Journal of Tropical Medicine* (London). I also sent a case suffering from this grievous malady to the parasitologist of the Union Medical College in Peking (Rockefeller Foundation) but he wrote saying that he had not been able to find the organism. The reason for this is probably found in the method of preparation of the specimen. If the blood film is dried and stained in the ordinary way, as is malaria, it is not easy to detect owing to adhesive qualities, and consequent difficulty in getting even distribution on the glass slide. The secret is to use a warm stage, and to examine the films wet; transferred direct from the patient to the microscope.

For purpose of study, I took an advanced case of this disease into hospital. Unfortunately he died soon after admission, and on his friends being informed they arranged to come for his body early on the following morning.

But this presented unusual difficulties. I was most anxious to make a post-mortem examination, and this quick removal gave me barely time to make the necessary preparations. The autopsy could only be done secretly, owing to the superstitions which exist in the Chinese mind associated with interference with the body after death. Serious trouble might be stirred up among the relatives and friends if my clandestine proceedings should come to light. However, the case was unique and of absorbing interest, and Dr Lei and I both felt justified in taking big risks in the cause of Science.

Again, the question arose – 'Where, under cover of night, could our dark deed be perpetrated?' We had no mortuary in which to conduct post-mortem examinations; the only place that offered was a ramshackle little out-house used as a stable for the pet donkey on which my small son rode daily to school. This dilapidated structure was hardly fit even for this purpose; but we had no alternative. Accordingly, about midnight, with the help of two trusty assistants, a rough table was erected in our improvised morgue. The next step, to bring out the body and convey it on a stretcher across the compound, was the most critical of all. But all was quiet in the hospital at that late hour, and it was accomplished without being observed and without arousing suspicion. So far, so good. An oil lamp in the hut afforded sufficient illumination, and all rays of light from this source were excluded from penetrating to the outside. The conduct of the donkey was exemplary, but as he was apt to get in the way it became necessary to tether him well to one side. We were now ready to begin, though feeling very much like guilty conspirators. I will not enter into technical details,

206

but only to remark that, as was to be expected, the liver had borne the brunt of the disease. It was enormously enlarged, and on removal was found to weigh 16 lbs.

The sewing-up of the cadaver was done neatly and carefully so as to give as little offence as possible in case of exposure. When laid in the coffin which had been provided, and decently covered, there was nothing to excite suspicion. By the time the relatives called in the morning all was in readiness for removal. No complaints were subsequently made, nor was there any trouble of any kind.

Microscopic sections taken from the liver afterwards showed that the substance of the organ had been largely replaced by a prodigious overgrowth of fibrous tissue, a change which denoted the presence of a powerful irritant in the blood. No doubt this irritant was provided by the toxins generated by the parasite; but how this minute protozoal organism gains an entrance into its human host, whether by the agency of some biting fly or otherwise, we were never able to determine.

Among the most difficult of our medical cases were the victims of the morphia habit. Though we did what we could to mitigate their sufferings while breaking free of the drug, the craving at times became so intense as to unbalance the mind and lead to acts of desperation. One of my last cases was that of a young fellow in foreign dress, who spoke English better than he did Chinese, having been educated in America. He was the first I had seen; spending several dollars daily in repeated injections. His system was saturated with morphia. The very first night in hospital he broke loose and escaped through one of the windows. Several weeks later I was called to see this youth at his home. He was then very ill with pneumonia; having drifted about the streets very insufficiently clad. He was removed to a private ward in the hospital, and actually recovered. As the fever subsided the old craving for morphia returned. When not under the influence of powerful sedatives he had to be tied to the bed to prevent him doing injury to himself and others, and to prevent attacks on the windows, the most accessible of which had to be boarded up. His talk was wild and incoherent and reflected his deranged mentality. One has to come into contact with these cases to appreciate the appropriateness of the term 'morpho-maniac'. Gradually the craving left him. The very thought of reverting to the drug became repellent. Before he left his mind had resumed the normal, he was enjoying the illustrated papers, taking a new interest in life, and determined that he had done with morphia for good. We lost sight of him after this, and have no knowledge of his subsequent history.

Cases of suicide were brought to the hospital not infrequently. As in the south I found that the chief agents employed were strong nitric acid and opium. Occasionally phosphorus, removed from matches, was used; also a certain kind of poisonous fly, and even, so I was informed, the dung of a serpent. In most cases there had been a quarrel, and revenge was usually the motive. In the Chinese view a disembodied spirit wields much greater power than when still imprisoned in the body – power to torment his enemy, and to bring upon him misery and disaster. Moreover if it be, as it so often is, a law case, the magistrate would come down heavily on the surviving litigant as having driven his adversary to extremes and been the cause of his death.

An unusual case was that of a boy in foreign employment who was much attached to his mistress. His relations were old dismissed servants of the house, and, as is not infrequently the case with dismissed servants in China, they sought to wreak their vengeance on their former employers. The habits of the household were well known. House-keeping money was kept in a certain place. The youth was to steal this and bring it to his friends. In this way they would be avenged for their dismissal, and would secure a big haul at the same time.

But the lad, usually so subservient to his elders, refused. He was bullied and threatened, and at length brought them a few dollars pilfered from a fellow servant. But this did not satisfy them. They determined now to obtain their revenge in another way. They would make the youth commit suicide, and would lay his dead body on the door-step of the hated foreigners. This would cause them great trouble, and the boy's departed spirit would haunt them.

Accordingly they forced the lad to swallow the contents of eight boxes of phosphorus matches. Then in a dying condition he was taken by night and laid at the front door of the house. Here he was discovered by his mistress. The latter, in great distress, brought him to the hospital. We could not save him, however, and he died soon after admittance.

At the end of the daily clinic there were always the beggars to be seen. They were usually in rags, and in an indescribable condition of dirt and disease; and some, like Lazarus, covered with sores. The offensive odour emanating from them, especially in the hot weather, was almost insupportable, even to my assistants, accustomed as they were to all sorts of evil smells in their native streets. We could not pretend to be very enthusiastic about admitting some of these cases, but it was remarkable how like ordinary patients they looked after a bath and a suit of clean pyjamas had done their transforming work. Their own clothing, not only filthy but alive, had to be consigned to the incinerator, and a fresh rig-out supplied to the patient when he left. This we were able to do by virtue of a special fund originated by Dr Lei for this purpose, and subscribed to by friends and former patients.

Hospital work represents not only an active warfare against disease but also a constant fight against dirt. The latter, in our old cramped buildings, and in the absence of so many modern conveniences, was apt to become wearisome. Nevertheless, our wards though old were warm and comfortable. Patients settled down quickly, were inclined to be sociable, and enjoyed each other's company. For many it was the first occasion on which they had been released, for a time, from the grinding struggle for existence. They were easily pleased and entertained. Sometimes lantern talks were given in the evenings, and such were always regarded as special treats. Help was also given by the hospital Evangelist to those who wished to learn to read. While lying in bed many had what was probably the first opportunity of their lives to learn to recognise their own Chinese characters. Each was given a small book presenting in large clear type the 600 ideograms in most common use. Some would commit to memory as many as twenty in a day; which meant that the 600 could be mastered in a month – the average length of stay in hospital. It is surprising how much reading can be done in Chinese if one is familiar with a few hundred characters; and having made a good start they felt encouraged, after leaving us, to go on and keep adding to their stock.

Sometimes the routine work would be seriously affected by widespread calamity. We had seen the floods break out from the swollen rivers in the south, inundating whole tracts of country, and, encroaching on the cities, convert the streets into canals. It was the same in the north. The effect of flood-water steadily rising in the public thoroughfares of Tientsin, so that all traffic had to be carried on in sampans, was, naturally, greatly to cut down our out-patient attendance; but it did not interfere much with the in-patient work as our ward floors were just above flood level.

It was otherwise with famine and civil war. These brought additional patients to our gates in the guise of starving refugees; or severely wounded country-folk whose only offence had been an attempt to protect their own property. With regard to famine goodly sums of money were raised, and much relief work undertaken, by foreigners resident in China. Many gave up their ordinary duties in order to go into the famine areas and supervise the distribution of rice. The reports they brought back as to the terrible condition of the starving people were harrowing in the extreme. After one very serious period of famine, some of us, by the courtesy of the Chinese Government, were the recipients of a decoration as delightfully ingenious as it was unexpected. It is in the form of a ribbon, with cloisonné pendant representing a sheaf of corn, and it is known as 'The fifth Order of the Most Excellent Crop!'

It will have been gathered from what I have said about the medical work in Tientsin how badly we needed a new hospital. The buildings had long seen their best days. And yet the work continued to increase. During our last year in China (1922) it had become impossible for Dr Lei and me to attend properly to the multitude of sick people. In that year there were 37,671 out-patient attendances (an average of 139 per clinic); and the number of operations performed under a general anaesthetic reached 1,211. We were terribly handicapped for want of space. We needed a larger waiting-hall for the patients, new and better wards, and up-to-date operating theatre, a good clinical laboratory, isolation wards, and more suitable accommodation for the assistants.

It was inevitable, therefore, that during our last year in Tientsin my

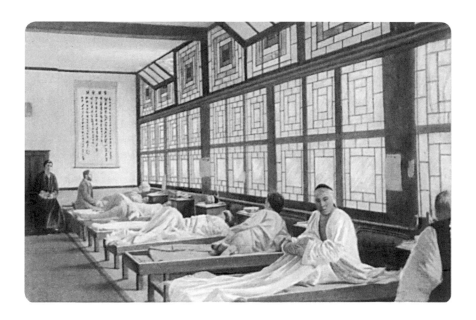

*Patients on a ward at the Mission hospital.*

thoughts should be very much occupied with the scheme for pulling down the old buildings and erecting a spacious, modern hospital in their place. We had the ground, but we lacked sufficient funds. A subscription list was started, and this was generously supported by the foreign community and by wealthy Chinese. I went ahead with the preparation of plans. But, apart from the difficulty of raising the very large sum required, delays arose from one cause or another, and we were never destined to see the new buildings. We returned home on furlough early in 1923, and my wife's ill-health precluded our return. But my successor, in due course, brought the scheme to full realisation, and, up to the time of the Japanese invasion, a great work, more extensive than ever, was being carried on in the new Mackenzie Memorial Hospital.

# Conclusion

In the foregoing pages I have written of China as I knew her; and I feel I can claim that, so far as it goes, I have given a true picture of the country and of the people during the early years of this century. I have faithfully recorded also my own personal experiences, though, for the sake of convenience and of giving the true local colour, I have not felt obliged to adhere to strict veracity in details and non-essentials. I have no doubt that fundamentally China is the same today, although superficially she is undergoing a transformation which is truly astonishing. The age-long slumber has been rudely interrupted. The consequences of the anti-foreign upheaval, known as the Boxer Rising, gave the Sleeper a nasty jolt; and a decade later, the anti-dynastic Revolution boiled up which brought the effete rule of the Manchus to an end. Finally in 1937 came the unprovoked onslaught of Japan. This, more than any other factor, accounts for the modernistic changes which in recent years have taken place in the country.

China, like Britain, has fought alone, with great courage and tenacity, against an enemy vastly superior in material strength. Concurrently with this militant courage a new spirit has arisen, and a new thirst for knowledge and progress. Gone for ever is the superior attitude of contempt for the foreigners. On the contrary his help is eagerly sought. Preoccupied as the Central Government is with military strategy and the task of winning the war, far-reaching national schemes are afoot for educational expenses, for development of the country's mineral wealth, for revival of native industries, for freer communications, and for increased transport facilities.

The war has knit all elements of the people together as nothing else could have done, and this unity has engendered a spirit of lively

*Dr Peake some years after his return to England.*

patriotism and co-operation hitherto unknown. I write this in the 9th year of China's gallant fight for freedom. The end is not yet, but it is not in doubt; and when she has emerged victorious the work of material and spiritual reconstruction (if internal discord can be averted) will be taken up again with enhanced enthusiasm.

No one who has lived long in China and closely observed her people can have failed to be impressed by certain characteristic virtues which appear to be a common inheritance. The ethical teachings of her sages have permeated the national mind and conscience for many centuries. Filial piety, reverence for their elders and teachers, correctness of conduct, and courtesy, are instilled into the child's mind from the earliest days and influence his whole future. The hard life of so many of the people has laid a substratum of endurance, patience, and industry. Upon this solid foundation the noble edifice of the Christian Faith is slowly rising.

When we remember China's great natural wealth, her immense population, and her potential qualities of mind and spirit, we cannot doubt the value of her contribution when she takes her place on an equal footing with the great nations of the world.[43]

The End

---

43 [ECP] Since I wrote these words the war has come to an end. The Japanese have been defeated and have vanished. But a new enemy has arisen within China's own borders in the guise of Communism, and her foes, activated by a great foreign Power, are they of her own household. The civil war now being staged has come as a sad blow to the earlier hopes of peace and progress.

# INDEX